# Ruby Ann's
# Down Home Trailer Park
# Cookbook

# Ruby Ann's
# Down Home Trailer Park
# Cookbook

## Ruby Ann Boxcar

CITADEL PRESS
Kensington Publishing Corp.
www.kensingtonbooks.com

The following are trademarks of their respective owners, who do not endorse this book:

Velveeta, Spam, Cocoa Puffs, Dr Pepper, Bisquick, Cheez Whiz, Miracle Whip, Jell-O, Mad Dog 20/20, 7 Up, Hot Damn, Crisco, Oreo, RC Cola, Red Hots, and Lipton


CITADEL PRESS BOOKS are published by

Kensington Publishing Corp.
850 Third Avenue
New York, NY 10022

All Kensington titles, imprints, and distributed lines are available at special quantity discounts for bulk purchases for sales promotions, premiums, fund-raising, educational, or institutional use. Special book excerpts or customized printings can also be created to fit specific needs. For details, write or phone the office of the Kensington special sales manager: Kensington Publishing Corp., 850 Third Avenue, New York, NY 10022, attn: Special Sales Department, phone 1-800-221-2647.

Citadel Press and the Citadel logo are trademarks of Kensington Publishing Corp.

Photos by Ruby Ann's husband Dew

First printing: May 2002

10  9  8  7  6  5  4  3

Printed in the United States of America

ISBN 0-8065-2349-2

Library of Congress Control Number: 2001099779

# *Dedication*

I want to give all thanks and praise to God (the Baptist one of course)! I also have to thank my family for all their love, support, and good cookin'. I can't forget the man who looked at this simple country gal and saw his personal Pamela Lee love doll! In the same breath, let me thank his Momma for not makin' him wear his glasses all the time as a young boy. I love you, Dew!

I've got to throw out a big thanks to Ms. Amy and her pet slug Slimy, who works at the Blue Whale Strip Club with my sister, Donna Sue. I could never have done this without your proofreadin'. Keep up your act with Slimy. I've seen strippers use snakes, but you're the first person that I know of who uses a slug.

Thanks to Mr. Howard Way of Fairview, Oklahoma, who taught a young up-and-comin' star that money can buy love ($5 and some car change to be exact).

A special thanks to my personal Porter Wagoner, my vocal coach, Mr. Randal Vance Powell (The American Tenor) who always believed in me. By the way, Mr. Powell, eight inches long and one inch around *is still a pencil* regardless of what state you might live in.

And I have to thank one of Donna Sue's old boyfriends, Mr. Curtis Moore, who taught me that the zippers on cheap luggage can and will bust open, leavin' all your private items all over the airport luggage conveyer belt for God and total strangers to see.

Last, but not least, thank you to the Florida Boys and Mrs. Vestal Goodman for givin' us fine inspirational songs like "Jubilee" and "Looking for a City".

God Bless y'all!

# Contents

# *Foreword*

For those of you who have never had the chance to see Ruby Ann Boxcar perform or who know little about her, we, her loving friends and fans, offer the following brief bio.

Ruby Ann Boxcar was born, raised, and someday in the far distant future hopes to die in a trailer home in her native Pangburn, Arkansas. A graduate of the Pangburn High School, Ruby Ann went on to obtain a cosmetologist license from the Pangburn Academy of Beauty and Horse Shoeing. Ms. Boxcar's nonacademic achievements include being crowned Miss Feeder Hog Junior Division at the Arkansas State Fair, president and founder of the Sweat Scarves of Elvis Fan Club, treasurer for the Baptist Association of Baptized Ladies (BABL), co-chairwoman of the Pangburn Democratic League, and board member of the High Chaparral Trailer Park residence committee. For her food entries in both the county and state fairs, Ms. Boxcar has received 38 first-place blue ribbons, a handful of second-place red ribbons, and some cheap third-place yellow ribbons, which she has thrown in a box somewhere.

At the tender age of 27, with her friends pushing behind her, she climbed up on a stage and has been wowing audiences with her tempting vocal talents and natural beauty ever since. When not on the road entertaining or jet setting with her famous friends, Ruby Ann and her husband, Dew, call the pink, custom-made, two-story, double-wide trailer parked in lot #18 their home. They also keep a simple custom-made quad-wide trailer (two double-wide trailers bolted together) in the good part of Commerce City, Colorado, for escaping the hot Arkansas summer months. Whether she is at home or on the road, Ruby Ann always enjoys participating in four of her favorite hobbies; singing, cooking, gossiping, and eating.

# Introduction

Hello, Ruby Ann Boxcar here! Bein' a well-known temptress of song, confidante to the jet set, former beautician extraordinaire, and world traveler, I always tend to find myself eatin' in a whole lot of high-class restaurants and fancy homes. You can't begin to imagine some of the things that have been in my mouth! In all fairness, let me just say that some of the eatin' was good. As for the majority of what I was served, well, I wouldn't have fed it to a dog! I kid you not! I wouldn't have given that food to a crippled beggar in India in fear that after one bite he would get up and hit me with his crutch! Lord, was it nasty! Now as sure as I say that, I know that a few of y'all would probably find that food tasty, and that's just fine. "To each his own," as I always say. But for a small-town gal with a down home trailer park palette, eatin' most of those dishes out of kindness was pure hell. Maybe I'm just spoiled when it comes to food. After all, I have been blessed by growin' up with a momma and a Me-Ma that can cook. Lord knows our trailer was always full of blue ribbons from both the Arkansas state and county fairs. As a matter of fact, my momma still enters one or two of her delightful dishes, and she always manages to take first place. And my dear old Me-Ma, God bless her soul, was always poppin' somethin' into the oven. Hell, I'm sure that precious woman would still be cookin' to this day if I hadn't finally hauled her butt into a nursin' home.

There just ain't nothin' like good trailer park cookin'! I know that for some of y'all this is hard to believe. It seems like every time I tell this to people, they always think that I'm kiddin'. I remember one evenin' after eatin' an awful dinner at one of them snooty French New York restaurants, my dear friends Jackie O., may she rest in peace, and Luciano Pavarotti were at each other's throats over which style of cookin' was the best. She was goin' on about French food while he insisted, rather vocally, that it was Italian. Well, not bein' one to hold her tongue for very long, I finally told 'em that they were both wrong. "There just ain't nothin' like good trailer park cookin'," I toned in. They stopped, looked at each other, and broke into laughter. "Fine," I told 'em, "just wait till we get back to Jackie's place, and then we'll see who's a laughin'!" Just as soon as Jackie unlocked the door, I hit the kitchen. Within no time I had cooked up a dessert that's a staple in every trailer dweller's diet. Needless to say, after one bite of my tomato soup cake they were forced to eat their words about trailer park cuisine. By the time Luciano and I had said our goodnights to Jackie and headed off to our separate hotel rooms (I am married after all), the once doubtin' friends had forced me to hand over the recipe for my tomato soup cake (which is included in this book). They, like many others, have found that when it comes to trailer park cookin', the proof is in the puddin' (Ruby Ann Boxcar's Dirt Bag Puddin' to be exact)!

There are three things that trailer park women are good at: holdin' our liquor, jackin' our hair to Jesus, and cookin'. Even when we get so old that the liquor runs right through us and there ain't any more hair left to jack or tease up, we can still cook up a meal like there's no tomorrow! Yes, bein' able to slam together a great-tastin' meal with whatever happens to be in the fridge is somethin' that's in our blood. It's a gift that the Almighty has seen fit to bestow on us common folk. It's like I told his Holiness, Pope John Paul II, durin' one of my many requested visits to the Papal Palace, "This Old Rugged Cross cake with sanctified sour cream frostin' is goin' to knock that beanie right off of your head." We trailer folk know that our cookin' is good, and we're doggone proud of it! You see, trailer park cookin' is more than just a way of preparin' a meal. It also happens to be a tool of comfort, which we folks turn to in times of need. Your son's been arrested . . . whip out the skillet! Your husband's cheatin' on you . . . fire up the stove! A tornado's been spotted a few trailers down . . . grease up a pie pan! Or, God forbid, the bingo bus has broken down right outside your door, and your car won't start . . . put your dauber down, and crack open some eggs! Yes, dear reader, trailer park cookin' plays a very large role in our everyday lives. Heck, why do you think Wal-Mart carries 3XL- to 5XL-sized stretch pants and caftans? Cookin' is the backbone in the trailer park skeleton of life.

Over the years we folks have hoarded our recipes like tickets to a championship wrestlin' event. We ain't told anyone their contents, and in some cases, have even served TV dinners to visitin' outsiders just to keep our secrets within our own community. Sure we'll go on national television and air our dirty laundry, but when it comes to our cookin' we're tighter than Jimmy Swaggart's hands on a widow's checkbook. I, too, must confess of only sharin' my personal titillatin' concoctions with a few of my closest friends and clients. But the last time I had to eat one of them terrible meals that I spoke of at the beginnin', I turned to my husband, Dew, and told him that it was time to throw open the trailer park recipe vaults for all the world to enjoy. After all, why should we be the only ones to enjoy a good meal? It just ain't fair! So, here they are! Here are some of the finest dishes that you will ever put a fork or spoon to. I, however, can't take all of the credit. No, I must share a tiny bit of the spotlight with all the members of my family and the rest of the inhabitants of the trailer park where I live. I told my family and all of the other residents at the 20 Lot High Chaparral Trailer Park about my idea for this book. Many of 'em were happy to hand out their own recipes, which you will find on the followin' pages. And then there were others that flatly refused to give away their secrets, so I swiped 'em from the recipe holders durin' a visit while the hostesses were in the john. Seein' how the closest thing to a Barnes and Noble Bookstore in my hometown of Pangburn is the adult bookstore by the highway, and the last book the Pangburn Library purchased was *Valley of the Dolls,* I can safely pass these recipes on to you without fear of my amateur cat burglary of the recipe boxes bein' disclosed.

In order to give you more of a feel about where these recipes came from, I've included a little bit about all of the people that live in the High Chaparral Trailer Park along with a map that shows you where everyone lives. When I have talked to folks about the trailer park life, I've been surprised by all of the misconceptions about our homes. Many folks think that trailers are cheap tin cans with fake wood panelin' and pressed wood furniture. In some cases this is true, but you would be astonished at the modern trailer home. To prove this I've included a guided tour of my own trailer followin' this introduction. Yes, seein' how I make a damn good livin' bein' a star and all, my two-story double-wide trailer is a bit better than most, but you can still get an idea of what is on the market nowadays. And hopefully this will help to put an end to all of those trailer myths.

With all of that said, it is time to take a trip into the recipe world of the trailer park. In the words of a dear friend and fellow cook, "Boner petite!" (I still have no idea what those words have to do with cookin', but in my younger single days, I did go out with a guy that had one of those. Needless to say, we didn't go out on a second date!)

NOTE: There are a few things concernin' the recipes in this book that I would like to address.

*Many of the recipes tell you to use government cheese.** If you ain't receivin' cheese from the government, feel free to use whatever kind of cheese you like just as long as it's a hard cheese (Cheddar, Colby, etc.). You can use VELVEETA if you got that kind of money.

*Many of the residents in trailer parks are either inbreeds (none of my family mind you) or elderly and suffer medical conditions, so some of the dishes in this book may not be seasoned to your likin'.** Feel free to add more salt or pepper than the recipe requires.

*Don't be fooled into believin' that you can substitute ham for SPAM!** If you use any other meat you will lose the true flavor of the dish. If it calls for SPAM, use it!

*Don't let the ingredients frighten you!** Trust me when I say you'll be surprised at how good the dish will taste. Now, if you don't like a kind of food or drink to start off with then you won't like the dish. For example, if you hate apples then you won't like apple pie. But if you like apples and the recipe for potato soup tells you to put apples in it, don't worry about it. Just do what the recipe says, regardless of how crazy or weird it may sound.

**\*Every recipe in this here book is EDIBLE!** That is, every recipe other than the ones that where given to me by my Me-Ma. She's old and sometimes doesn't live in this world, if you know what I mean, but knowin' that she'll read this book, I had to include the recipes that she gave me. Don't worry, she won't read this paragraph. I'll mark it out with a black marker in her copy. Just remember that if a recipe has "Me-Ma" at the end of it, don't try to make it! You'll only get upset, and somebody might get hurt.

And now the traditional good feelin' corny recipe for life that must start off all down home cookbooks.

## HAPPINESS CAKE

**1 cup good thoughts**
**1 cup kind deeds**
**4 cups consideration for others**
**2 cups sacrifice**
**2 cups faults, well-beaten**
**3 cups forgiveness**
**Mix thoroughly addin' tears of joy, sorrow and sympathy, love and kindly service if needed. Fold in 4 cups of prayerful faith. Pour into your daily life and bake well with the heat of human kindness. Serve with a smile anytime, and it will satisfy the hunger of many souls.**
**—*AUTHOR UNKNOWN***

If that don't make you want to up and vomit, I've got some nude pictures of me that my husband, Dew, took while I was semi-comatose after a bout with some bad mail-ordered fish! To this day, even the slightest smell of seafood just turns my stomach and arouses my husband, Dew.

# *Chapter 1*

Standin' in front of our trailer are Trixy, me Ruby Ann,
Shady Lady, my husband, Dew, and Silver Fox.

# A Trailer Fit for a Queen

Yes, I've truly been blessed in my life. The Lord has seen fit to give me a good husband, many talents, tons of friends (famous and not), great family members, and a wonderful home. Because of my singin', I've been able to own a trailer that is fit for a queen. My two-story double-wide pink trailer home is not just a thing of beauty for all who see it, but it's also a shrine to fine livin'. As I stated in my introduction, many people who have never lived in a trailer home almost always have the wrong idea about 'em. They've bought into the myth that a home on wheels is nothin' but a cheaply constructed firetrap with bad decor and furniture. Needless to say, nothin' could be farther from the truth, and I feel that my home proves it.

I must point out and warn you that not everyone can have my kind of taste. As a matter of fact, one time while I was playin' canasta with Ralph Lauren, Bob Mackie, and Donna Karen, Ralph turned to me and said, "Ruby Ann, if everyone had taste like you, I think I can safely say the three of us would be broke." What he said was right. When it comes to somethin' like taste, God has seen fit to give it to just a few of us. And I feel like he also expects those of us whom he's blessed to share our gifts with others. That's one of the reasons why I'm always happy to give guided tours of my trailer home. By doin' this simple task, I always hope it'll help inspire visitors to reach for the best and not settle for less. Yes, I feel like I'm doin' God's work. So if you happen to see somethin' in my trailer home that you like, some color scheme or what have you, feel free to take my ideas and use 'em.

Seein' how my good friends Bill Clinton and Al Gore had been encouragin' the use of the Internet, I've decided to make this chapter an interactive one. In other words, you can take a personal tour of my trailer and stay as long as you want by simply goin' to my homepage. The other plus of this interactive page is you can share this tour with all your friends without havin' to loan 'em your book! With this in mind, start up your computer and surf over to www.rubyann.org to begin the official tour of me and my husband, Dew's, trailer home.

For some of y'all, this tour will be the first time you've ever had the chance to see the inside of a trailer other than on the news when they're showin' one that's been ripped apart by a twister. I hope that this tour has shed a little light into the world of trailer owners. Sure, our homes are different from the normal ones that have basements and are built into the ground, but maybe now you can see they're just as important to us as the typical home is to its owner. I hope that all of you enjoyed my home as much as me and my husband, Dew, enjoy it. And if you're ever up in these parts stop by and visit. Just remember, dear reader, as the French say, "Me Casa, you Casa!"

# *Chapter 2*

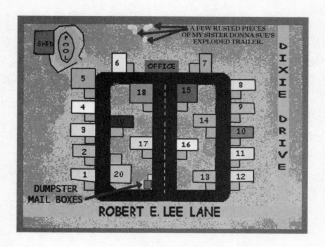

# The High Chaparral Trailer Park's "Who's Who" and Where the Heck They Live

01. Tammy Cantrell and children
02. Anita Biggon
03. Mr. and Mrs. Hubert and Lois Bunch
04. Mr. and Mrs. C. M. and Nellie Tinkle
05. Mr. and Mrs. Cecil Boxcar (my Momma and Daddy)
06. Donna Sue Boxcar (my older sister)
07. Mr. and Mrs. Ben and Dora Beaver
08. Lulu Bell Boxcar (my niece)
09. Mr. and Mrs. Harland and Juanita Hix and children
10. Ollie White
11. Mr. and Mrs. Kyle and Kitty Chitwood
12. Sister Bertha Fay Bluemoker
13. Mr. and Mrs. Mickey Ray and Connie Kay and Wanda Kay
14. Dottie Lamb and her daughter, Opal Lamb
15. Donny Owens and Kenny Lynn
16. Momma Ballzak (my husband's momma)
17. Mr. and Mrs. Marty and Mable Scaggs
18. Me and my husband, Dew
19. Mr. and Mrs. Jimmy and Jeannie Janssen
20. Mr. and Mrs. Elmer and Lovie Birch

I just wanted to thank Mrs. Willa May Buttrim and her first hour art class at the Pangburn High School for their fine charcoal pencil drawin' of the trailer park. And in return for the map drawin', I promised Willa May that I would plug her and her husband, Bobby's, store. So just remember, when you're lookin' for the lowest prices and highest quality in adult pornography and accessories, stop by the Come and Go adult bookstore down by the highway. Willa May says, "Don't forget to take a peek at their newly added secondhand pleasure toy bin for great savin's in all your bedroom needs." That's the Come and Go adult bookstore, open from 4 P.M. to midnight every day but Sunday. And don't forget to tell 'em Ruby Ann sent you for an additional 5% off all nonwrapped items!

# *Chapter 3*

Back row left to right; Momma Ballzak; me Ruby Ann; my husband, Dew;
Lulu Bell with her daddy in hand; Donna Sue's boyfriend, Dwight; Donna Sue;
and Daddy Boxcar. Seated left to right are Momma Boxcar and Me-Ma.

# *The Residents of the High Chaparral Trailer Park Lot by Lot*

## LOT #1

In lot #1 lives Tammy Cantrell (age 24) and her six bastard kids: Tammy (7), Dolly (6), Patsy (5), Conway (4), Reba (3), and Oakridge (2). When Tammy's granny passed away back in 1990, she left her trailer and her lot to Tammy in the will. A few months after she moved in, some trucker named Hank shacked up with her (we were all surprised that she was able to get a man in the first place). That gal has got some hips, if you know what I mean. It looks like she's tied a 50-lb. bag of flour on each thigh. And with those little breasts of hers, well, trust me, it ain't pretty; she looks like a gigantic bowlin' pin! Gettin' back to what I was sayin' about this trucker fella, he spent most of the time on the road, but when he was in town, there was always a fight goin' on in lot #1. If I had a dime for every time the police had come to that trailer durin' the first year she lived there, I'd have a third story on my trailer home by now. Oh, it was bad, all the fightin' and swearin'. After a few more months, he just packed up and left while she was at work in Searcy at the day-old Dolley Madison store. Needless to say, when she got back home that night you could hear the cryin' all the way in Little Rock. Bein' the good Baptist woman that I am, I called her to see if she wanted to talk. She said no, so I told her if she changed her mind to just let me know, but in the meantime would she try to keep the noise down. I could hardly hear the doggone TV! Six months later little Tammy Wynette Cantrell was born (she names her babies after the performers that are playin' on the radio at the time of conception). Hank showed up soon af-

11

ter, but only stayed for three or four weeks. Nine months later Dolly Parton Cantrell came into this world, and Hank showed up again. And then he was gone. Just like clockwork, she ends up producin' a baby every nine months after he visits. Just before she had her last kid, Oakridge Boys Cantrell, we at the First Baptist Church of Pangburn, which she also belongs to, took up an offerin' so she could get her tubes tied. It was either that or hire on another person to help watch her kids durin' church services. Every once in a while you'll still find a semi parked out along Robert E. Lee Lane, and you know Hank is back in town. Thanks to the fine, up-standin', God-fearin' folks in town, there won't be a souvenir of his visit nine months down the road.

## LOT #2

Anita Biggon (54) lives in lot #2. Anita and I grew up in the same trailer park together. We both went to school together and even used to chase the boys together. Heck, we did just about everything together when we were kids. After I graduated from the Pangburn Academy of Beauty and Horse Shoein', we both kind of went our separate ways. I was busy tryin' to make my career in the cosmetology world, and she shacked up with a beer distributor and moved to Fort Smith. The summer of 1989, she moved back in with her momma on lot #2, and started workin' as a cocktail waitress at the Three Cigarettes in the Ashtray Bar on 1st Street. By then I was already busy with my career as a star, so I didn't have time to run around with her like we had done as children. Her momma passed away back in 1993 after bein' run over by an out of control clown car at the circus, held every year durin' the Arkansas State Fair. She asked if I would do her momma's makeup for the funeral services, and of course I agreed. I had a heck of a time tryin' to cover up those tiny tire tracks on her forehead, but everybody said it was the best she'd ever looked. Anita and I spent more time together after her momma's passin', but with my out-of-town singin' engagements and all, we kind of drifted apart. We still see each other now and then at the Piggly Wiggly in Searcy or out by the entrance of the trailer park. Anita now owns the Three Cigarettes in the Ashtray Bar. Rumor has it she's plannin' on addin' a grill, so I might be seein' more of her in the near future. Let me tell you, this gal can cook!

# LOT #3

The trailer in lot #3 is home to Hubert (61) and Lois (60) Bunch. Both Hubert and Lois run the Taco Tackle Shack on the corner of Main Street and Plucket Drive. They've got some of the best Mexican food in Arkansas. My husband, Dew, says that they also have one of the largest bait and fishin' gear selections in this neck of the woods. The Bunchs are our newest residents in the High Chaparral Trailer Park. They moved here from a small town in Texas just five years ago. Hubert use to be a travelin' evangelist, and Lois would play the piano at his revival services. Lois says they met back in 1955 durin' a tent revival when Hubert was just startin' out in the ministry. It seems that she'd been havin' some pains in her chest, so she decided to go hear this new preacher at a tent revival her church was sponsorin'. She knew at the end of the service they usually invited the sick to come down to the front for prayer (it was an Assembly of God service). Sure enough, young Hubert asked anyone that was feelin' under the weather to come on down for a healin'. Lois got in line and waited for her turn for a miracle. After a little bit it was finally her turn. She says she told Hubert that she had been havin' pains in her chest so he asked her whereabouts. Durin' this little exchange, Lois noticed how handsome this young preacher was, and she couldn't help but instantly take a fancy to him. She told him that the pains were in the top of her chest, and Hubert placed his hand where she had located. Hubert said a prayer, the pains went away, and Lois went back to her seat so that the other people in line could receive their healin's. After the service Lois went home. She had been way too shy to say anything to Hubert, but she just couldn't get him out of her mind. So she went back the next night, and took her place in the line for prayer. This time when she came face to face with Hubert he looked at her and asked if the pains had come back in her chest. She couldn't believe he had remembered her from the night before, but she didn't know what she should say about why she was in the prayer line. Without thinkin' she said no, but that she was havin' a tinglin' in her left breast. Hubert put his manly hand on her breast and said a prayer. That night he stopped her and asked if she would like to go out for some coffee. They were married three days later and have been together ever since.

## LOT #4

Nellie (72) and C. M. (71) Tinkle rent out lot #4. The Tinkles along with my folks were one of the first families to move into the trailer park back in 1943. Nellie was my music teacher at Pangburn Elementary School where she worked until her retirement in 1976. C. M. worked for the Pangburn sanitation department until he retired along with Nellie. He was in charge of keepin' the fire burnin' at the town's garbage dump. Nowadays, C. M. and Nellie enjoy spendin' their time keepin' up with championship wrestlin'. They've traveled all across Arkansas, Missouri, and Oklahoma just to attend a match. The livin' room walls of their trailer are covered with autographs of all the wrestlers past and present.

Nellie's the organist at the First Baptist Church of Pangburn, and C. M. works the organ's wind pump. Our church has voted several times over the years in regards to buyin' a new organ, but the majority has always insisted on keeping the same old pump organ that was first installed back when the church was constructed in 1853. We've had to make many a repair to the old girl, but she still sounds great. Plus it does one's heart good to walk into the church on Sunday mornin' to find Nellie bent over the keyboard with C. M. pumpin' away.

## LOT #5

My momma, Imogene (72), and Daddy, Cecil (76), live in lot #5. As a matter of fact I grew up in lot #5. My late brother, Jack Daniel, God rest his soul, and my older sister, Donna Sue, both just babies at the time, moved with my folks to the trailer park when it first opened. Back then, Daddy was one of the few men still left in the area on account of World War II and all. He had tried to join the Army in 1941, but due to the fact that he had been born without index (trigger) fingers, the Army turned him down. My momma use to say if Daddy hadn't been born a freak, she might have lost him overseas. With the lack of men in the surroundin' counties, Daddy was able to get a ton of farmin' work, which paid real well. He and Momma saved up their money, and when the trailer park opened, they bought a little trailer and moved out from Grandpa and Granny Boxcar's storm shelter where they'd lived since they were married. After the war Daddy went to work for the old grain store, which used to be located right in the middle of what is now the highway exit goin' in to Pangburn. Of course, Momma stayed home and raised us kids. In 1958 Daddy rented out the old drugstore buildin' on the corner of Main Street and Jefferson Davis Blvd. in order to open up The Boxcar Nuts and Bolts Hardware Store. Daddy finally sold his business six years ago and is currently enjoyin' his retirement with Momma. Me and my husband, Dew, bought 'em the trailer (double-wide of course) that is currently parked in their lot for their 50th weddin' anniversary.

## THE TRAILER PARK POOL

Seein' how most of us have our own little turtle pools and a water hose, we don't use the provided pool much. Usually the only time you'll find us out by the pool is on the Fourth of July after all the goin's on in town are over. We all get together and roast weenies. Other than that, well, you might find some of the menfolk down by the pool in the evenin' huntin' frogs and drinkin' beer.

## LOT #6

My older sister, Donna Sue, (56), has her Wild Woman trailer parked in lot #6. Donna Sue has always been the sexpot in the family. Now don't get me wrong, I enjoy a good ride as much as the next gal, but my sister just has to have it all the time. Of course we don't talk about that in front of Momma or Daddy, but I think they know she's a slut. After all, the only thing between their trailer and hers is the cement pathway to the pool! They ain't stupid people. She's 56 years old and has a new boyfriend every other week. Heck, they know she meets these guys at the Blue Whale Strip Club in Searcy where she strips. They found that out by mistake 12 years ago when Daddy and Momma took my Pa-Pa and Me-Ma there thinkin' it was a new seafood and steak restaurant. Can you imagine? Thinkin' you're a goin' to have a fancy seafood and steak dinner only to find your over-weight 44-year-old daughter up on a stage bumpin' and grindin' in nothin' but a pair of pasties and a stretched-out thong! Luckily neither my Pa-Pa nor my Me-Ma could see very well. They thought she was one of those me-chanical bulls that customers can ride for free. Well, they were halfway right! In any case, my folks don't talk about it even when the subject is brought up, and trust me, it comes up a lot in the trailer park. What do you expect when she walks around in nothin' but a teddy, leavin' her curtains and trailer door open for any man that might be headed to the pool to hunt frogs? Oh, well, she is family after all.

## THE OFFICE

This is the same small brick office that my momma and daddy went into when they signed their very first lot-rental agreement back in 1943. Back then it was called the F. D. R. Trailer Court. "Park" didn't come into the name until 1971 when it was bought out by a company in Texas and re-named the Richard Nixon Memorial Trailer Park. This name change really upset a lot of the residents. Most of us were dyed-in-the-wool Democrats who couldn't stand President Nixon. Those few registered Republicans who lived in the park were also unhappy about the new name. They thought the Memorial part was offensive, seein' how Nixon wasn't dead at the time and was still in office. Well, nobody in Texas gave a rat's left butt cheek about what a trailer park full of idiots in Arkansas thought about the new name, so we put together a plan of action. Both Democrat and Republican trailer owners alike got together and decided to stop up all the sewers. We were flushin' anything and everything that we could find down our toilets in an attempt to make the trailer park owners spend money to have the septic tanks unclogged. Not only was this plan good for the people in the park to show their lack of personal like for the new Texas owners, but Dink, the town plumber, was pretty happy about the whole idea as well. He was out there with a smile uncloggin' sewers every day, sometimes two or three times a day for that matter. This went on for about a month until the owners sent out letters statin' that we were hereby responsible for any plumbin' cost due to clogs in our septic tanks. Our current plan of rebellion against the Texas owners had been thrown into the toilet with that letter, so to speak, but don't get me wrong by thinkin' we took this sittin' down. We had only begun to fight! One of the Janssen twins came up with the idea of flushin' little sticks of dynamite with waterproof fuses down the toilets. Before the dynamite could ignite, it would be safely away from your trailer home and into the septic tank. There was just enough TNT in these little things to cause the explosive gases that were already in the septic tanks to ignite. It was a brilliant idea! My daddy, who had the dynamite in stock at his hardware store, and some of the other men in the trailer court all chipped in and bought what we needed. We all decided to start the plan on October 31, and called in Dink to let him know what was goin' on. Since his steady income for uncloggin' septic tanks had completely dropped off after we got that letter, he was more than happy to make up some story about why the septic tanks were blowin' up. After all, since the owners were in Texas, they'd have to buy the new tanks from him, plus pay him for puttin' 'em in. At 7 P.M. October 31st the plan started commencin'. Before the owners knew what had happened, there was sewage flyin' everywhere. Mind you, it wasn't pleasant at first. We hadn't thought about havin' a blowin' up schedule on that first night, which would have scattered the explosions throughout the evenin'. We also had managed to forget that October 31st was Halloween. When those tanks started explodin', there were kids trick or treatin' throughout the trailer park. It was terrible! One second you had Casper the Friendly Ghost and Cinderella standin' at your trailer door, and before you could whistle "Dixie" the poor little tykes had turned into two tiny pieces of candy-seekin' poop. Of course a little flying human waste didn't stop these trailer park kids from trick or treatin'. Needless to say, with all the blastin' goin' on, everybody's trees were unintentionally T.P.'ed that Halloween night. The next day we came up with a blastin' schedule. The owners in Texas were mad as all get out! But what could they do? After all, this happens to old septic tanks when the weather changes from summer to fall. Or at least that's what Dink had 'em believin'! Before the month was over, the Texans had sold the trailer park to Pangburn's own Ben and Dora Beaver, and the explodin' septic tanks stopped.

The only casualty of war was when my sister, Donna Sue, had come home one late evenin' three sheets to the wind. After stumblin' into her tiny trailer home, she used the bathroom, and in her state of mind, decided to show how loyal she was to the cause of her fellow trailer dwellers by includin' a stick of dynamite with everything that was already in the toilet. Well, when she went to flush, the toilet clogged up from all the paper, which she'd drunkenly used. She managed to focus long enough to find the plunger, but just when she began to use it, the dynamite exploded! Before she knew what hit her, that little trailer she called home was layin' in pieces over in a nearby field, and she was hangin' bare naked upside down in a walnut tree by her panty hose. The sheriff later said that there wouldn't have been as much damage if she hadn't had her cabinets filled with liquor bottles.

After the Beavers took over, they decided to let the residents of the trailer park come up with a new name. Bein' the celebrity that I am, I was appointed chair of the nomination committee. Everybody turned in a name, and we picked the best two, High Chaparral Trailer Park and Pangburn Trailer World. Each trailer was then given a vote for which one of the two names they liked the best (the committee decided to go ahead and let Donna Sue vote even though her trailer was blown to smithereens and officially out of the park). High Chaparral Trailer Park won hands down. Instead of havin' to pay to take down the old sign on the office buildin', the Beavers decided to leave the Trailer Park section up, and hang the High

Chaparral on top of the rest of it. Ben and Dora Beaver sold the park in 1994 to their daughter Ima, who lives in Hot Springs, and her roommate, Lizzy Bein. Ima and Lizzy asked Ben and Dora to stay on and run the business for them. They agreed and now occupy lot #7 rent-free.

## LOT #7

As I just mentioned, this lot belongs to Ben and Dora Beaver. These are two of the nicest Pangburnians that you'll ever meet (next to me and my husband, Dew, of course). They also happen to be the proud owners of the only store in town that sells alcohol. So if you ever happen to pass this way, make sure to wet your whistle at Beaver Liquors. Currently they're holdin' wine appreciation classes right in the store in an attempt to introduce these small-town folks to a few of the finer, tasteful things in life. They meet every Tuesday night, so those of us good Baptists, who might happen to actually get a bit tipsy only have to wait until the followin' evenin' to confess at Wednesday night's church service. If these Beaver Liquors "Taste the Difference" classes keep goin' over as well they are, we might even wind up gettin' a PBS channel.

## LOT #8

My niece Lulu Bell Boxcar (33) has her little trailer parked in lot #8. This lot used to belong to my late brother, Jack Daniel. Of course after he and his witch of a wife, Blanche, divorced back in 1990, she got the trailer, which she quickly hitched up and hauled off to Lamar, Arkansas. So he got to keep the lease on lot #8. Rather than buy a new trailer, Jack Daniel decided to move to Dallas in an attempt to find a backer for his new full-size plastic molded toilet seat cover. Of course we were all behind him in his endeavor. After all, his invention was ingenious: a full-size plastic molded toilet seat cover that you placed over any standard public bathroom toilet seat. You didn't have to worry about it blowin' off just when you start to set down like them darn paper ones.

Anyways, Lulu Bell went to live with my momma and daddy. Lulu Bell is, shall we say, special like in Special Olympics. We all thought it would be better if she lived with family members rather than to move with her daddy. And her momma, the dog that she is, didn't want anything to do with her. That's one of the reasons why it was so hard to tell her that her father had been killed. It seems that while he was drivin' his Moped to a meetin' with a prospective backer, the truck he was behind quickly stopped and the back door popped open. The truck's entire shipment of women's size 12 and 13 one-inch pumps flew out of the truck and onto my brother's helmetless head, killin' him instantly. The doctor said if they'd only been size 7 or 8, he might still be alive today. He left Lulu Bell his lease on lot #8, the patent on his invention, and his old collection of baseball cards. Luckily durin' one of my singin' engagements in Russia, I was able to find a backer, and Lulu Bell sold her daddy's toilet seat cover idea to him for $20,000. She took a portion of the money, bought a little trailer, and parked it in lot #8. She's doin' fine out on her own. Lulu Bell even started her own Billy Ray Cyrus fan club a couple years ago and is workin' on puttin' together a Kathy Lee Gifford fan club.

She decided to have her daddy cremated, but she could never decide on an urn she liked. So, currently she keeps his ashes in a zipped freezer bag, which she stores in what we call the "urn of the month." One month the urn might be an old instant mashed potato box or a hot chocolate container. This may sound fun, but it can have terrible consequences. To this day I can't drink a glass of tea on account of the time my Me-Ma was trailer sittin' for a travelin' Lulu Bell. When I stopped by to make sure the old lady was fine, she offered me a glass of cold ice tea. It didn't take long for me to discover that she had made the "tea" with two scoops from a Lipton Instant Ice Tea jar, which happened to house the remains of my dearly beloved brother. Well, he was never all there in the first place!

## LOT #9

Juanita Hix (29) and her husband, Harland (29), reside in lot #9 with their two girls, Harlinda (11) and Bonita (9). Both Juanita and Harland

work at the Piggly Wiggly in Searcy. She's a cashier, and he holds the job ti-
tle of head sacker. Juanita and Harland attended Pangburn High School. She
was president of their class, student council, French and Spanish club, the de-
batin' team, vice-president of the science club, and valedictorian. Harland
was the official towel boy for the Pangburn High School football team four
years in a row. Accordin' to Harland's momma, Mertle, Juanita and Harland
hardly spoke to each other while they were in school. As she understands it,
they had their first real conversation durin' the party Juanita was throwin' at
the Big Balls Bowling Alley in celebration of her acceptance into Vassar Col-
lege. Harland was workin' his summer job as shoe boy at the bowlin' alley
that evenin'. Juanita and her handful of friends were bowlin' and drinkin'
Chocolate Soldiers and vodka that they had snuck in. They were partyin' all
the way up to closin' time. Harland says that Juanita refused to leave with her
friends. She told 'em she wasn't goin' anywhere until she'd had her way with
Harland. Juanita usually butts in around here, and adds that the last thing
she remembered on that night was tryin' to pick up a split before blackin'
out. In any case, she woke up the next mornin' bare butt naked lyin' in a
bowlin' lane gutter with Harland. They married in July, and their first daughter, Harlinda, was born the followin' March. Juanita never went to Vassar,
but she did attend several Vo-Tech classes. You can find Juanita drivin' the
bookmobile on Sunday afternoons, while Harland works his second job as a
pin boy at the newly remodeled Great Big Balls Bowling Alley (they've added
two more lanes for a total of 5).

## LOT #10

Mrs. Ollie White (63) and her late husband, Orville, moved into lot #10
47 years ago when they were newlyweds. Ollie's been workin' as a cafeteria
cook at the Pangburn High School for almost as long. She has won the coveted Miss White County Hairnet Award for best school cafeteria cook in
White County more than six times over the years. The Pangburn Post Office employed Ollie's late husband, Orville, for the last 34 years of his life as
a letter carrier. As a matter of fact, he was workin' his rural route on the day

he died. While he was deliverin' free samples of COCOA PUFFS along with the rest of the normal mail, Orville's truck was attacked and overtaken by a wild pack of pigs. The cuckoo for COCOA PUFF pigs snorted poor Orville to death in their attempt to obtain the tiny boxes of chocolaty breakfast food. The postal department gave Orville a nice send-off, and Ollie received a letter of sympathy along with a lifetime supply of COCOA PUFFS from the company that makes 'em. Seein' how Ollie has been a widow for the past 12 years, she usually just brings home some of the leftovers from school for her nightly supper. So some of the recipes Widow White gave me are for groups of 50 or more. Just divide the ingredients by 10 and you shouldn't have any problems bakin' her dishes for your own family.

## LOT #11

Kitty (32) and Kyle (35) Chitwood pay the rent on lot #11. Kitty's the night clerk at the Gas and Smokes convenience store on Main Street and Turtle drive. She can really pull a good RC slushy. Kyle's the bartender at my old friend Anita's Three Cigarettes in the Ashtray Bar on 1st Street. Kitty doesn't mind the fact that Kyle's around attractive drunk women all night, just as long as he doesn't bring one of 'em home with him. The thing that does tick her off is when he comes home half cocked and ends up leavin' cans of opened beer all over the house. Most of 'em have only had a few swallows drank out of 'em. Kitty's not one to throw away somethin' (you ought to go into the Gas and Smokes and buy a hot dog while she's workin'). So she's come up with her own recipes that use leftover beer or other liquors that her husband hadn't finished. Surprisin'ly they're pretty doggone good! Kitty did give me some recipes that call for out-of-date sandwich meats and dairy products, but I left those out of this book.

## LOT #12

Lot #12 belongs to Bertha Fay Bluemoker (59), better known in these parts as Sister Bertha. Now if Baptists had nuns, Sister Bertha would be the first in line to sign up. She is devoted to the First Baptist Church of Pangburn and all that it stands for. My momma said that even as a little girl, Sister Bertha would carry around a Bible everywhere she went. Momma doesn't remember ever seein' her actually read the Bible, but she always had it with her. If you ever miss a Sunday mornin', Sunday night, or Wednesday night service, then you can bet a dollar to a doughnut Sister Bertha, with Bible in hand, will be on your doorstep faster than a bull on a cow. The only social activities that she takes part in are all church-related. Now, don't get me wrong. She won't try to save you, but she will tell you that you're goin' to Hell. And if you ain't Baptist, you better watch out for her! She and some of the other women of the church have got an observation group organized, kind of like a neighborhood watch, but only instead of crime, they're watchin' for sin. If you look like you might be doin' somethin' sinful, then these ladies make sure that everybody else in town knows what you were doin'. They also keep an eye out for strangers passin' through. I remember one time when a few Jehovah Witnesses decided to stop in Pangburn and go knockin' door to door. Sister Bertha jumped in her car and hunted 'em down. She came by my trailer and asked if I'd seen hide or hair of those "doggone ungodly heathen Watch Tower carryin' Jehovah Witnesses." When she did finally locate the poor souls, she informed 'em that this town was a Baptist town, and that they could peddle their satanic beliefs somewhere else. She then got in her car and, along with the rest of the women, followed 'em until they'd left the city limits.

But that's Sister Bertha for you. I do feel sorry for her. Every time a tornado comes this way it always manages to touch down, hit her trailer, and then disappear back into the clouds. It never hits or even damages any of the other trailers in the park, just hers. I can't even begin to tell you how many times she's had to buy a new one. Luckily her parents left her a good deal of money from the grain store they owned (the same one my daddy worked for). Seein' how she never upped and married (I don't know if that was by choice or fate), and she ain't got any family, she has to be sittin' pretty. Although I'm sure the First Baptist Church of Pangburn is mentioned somewhere in her will.

## LOT #13

Connie (36) and Mickey Ray Kay (37) have their trailer parked in lucky #13. Connie's our local Amway distributor, and Mickey Ray's a manager at the DR. PEPPER plant in Searcy. Mickey's momma, Wanda (64), also lives with 'em. She works in the restaurant area of town at the Dream Cream on 1st Street and Plucket Drive. Every time me and my husband, Dew, go in she always gives us an extra scoop on our cones for free.

Wanda and her daughter-in-law, Connie, have always hit it off. When Mickey and Connie go away to Branson or Silver Dollar City for a vacation, they take Wanda along with 'em. They're real good people. As a matter of fact, every Friday after he gets off work, Mickey always brings over a free case of DR. PEPPER for my husband, Dew. And Connie always makes sure to invite us over to their trailer when they're havin' a party or just for a game of Uno. The only bad thing is that Connie's always tryin' to either sell you somethin' or sign you up to work for Amway. Occasionally, I'll buy some Amway laundry detergent just to shut her up.

## LOT #14

Dottie Lamb (58) and her dog-ugly daughter, Opal (35), live in lot #14. They both run the Lamb Department Store on Main Street between Plucket Drive and Jefferson Davis Blvd., which her husband, Laverne, left her after his death. Laverne was a Dragon or a Wizard or somethin' or other with the local chapter of the Ku Klux Klan (my family never supported or had any affiliation with this group, so I'm not sure of the titles). In any case, he and Dottie had gone to Galveston, Texas, for a weeklong small-business seminar. While Laverne was attendin' workshops, Dottie would go across the border into Mexico to shop. In between classes, Laverne and Dottie would take advantage of the beautiful beaches and refreshin' waters. Back then in the early 60s none of us knew anything about sun blocks, so by the end of the week Laverne and Dottie had gotten a really deep dark tan under the hot Texas sun. When they finally made it back to Pangburn, they were runnin' so late

Laverne dropped Dottie off and headed out for one of his Klan meetin's with their Cadillac still packed to the brim with their luggage and Mexican items that Dottie had purchased. Laverne had always told his wife that he was meetin' with some of his friends to play poker. Secretly he was just goin' to change into his white robes when he got there. On his way to the meetin' some of his fellow members that were drivin' behind him mistook the tanned Laverne for a Hispanic man. They ran him off the road, pulled him out of the car, beat the heck out of him, and before he could say a word, they strung him up from a tree. It wasn't until the next day that they realized they'd killed their own leader. Dottie got the store and quite a bit of money. She also received a letter of sympathy from the Klan and from that day to this they only buy their white sheets from the Lamb Department Store.

## LOT #15

Donny Owens (43) and Kenny Lynn (33) share a double-wide trailer right across the street from me and my husband, Dew, in lot #15. They own the Times Gone By antiques store in Searcy. Both Kenny and Donny are members of the park's quiltin', macramé, and needlepoint clubs. Not only are they crafty, but these boys can play some real mean canasta! Neither one of 'em is married. Me and my husband, Dew, think it must have somethin' to do with their religious beliefs. They're very spiritual people. As a matter of fact, many a nights I've heard 'em prayin'. They get so into their prayers that you can hear 'em yellin' out, "Oh, God, yes," all the way across the street. Some of the girls and I think that they've taken a vow of celibacy seein' how we never see any women over at their trailer. Their sisters do come into town ever Halloween, but Kenny and Donny never seem to be around to introduce me to 'em. I've only seen 'em from a distance, but they're always dressed really nice. I did ask Donny about 'em one day, and he said that their siblin's are models, which makes sense seein' how all the models that I've ever met are also tall and big boned.

Thanks to these two boys our trailer park float entry won first prize at last years annual Pangburn Christmas parade. Our float was entitled A

Christmas Somewhere over the Rainbow. Kenny and Donny designed the whole thing by themselves. They had a yellow brick road that started at the back of the float and led up to a miniature cardboard Emerald City. A big rainbow with a small papier-mâché Santa Claus flyin' over it in his sleigh was propped up above the miniature city. Some of us from the trailer park rode on the float dressed up like Oz characters (I was Glenda the Good Witch). Needless to say, a good time was had by all.

# LOT #16

Me and my husband, Dew, moved his momma into lot #16 after her first heart attack eight years ago. Momma Ballzak (72) (I kept my maiden name when me and my husband, Dew, married because I was already established in the entertainment profession) has had three more heart attacks since we moved her closer to us, but she is doin' just fine, thank you. After her last big one we were able to talk her into cuttin' down to just five packs of Lucky Strikes a day. With my talents, I've been able to make quite a lot of money over the years, but she refuses to let us support her. She won't quit her cashier's job at The Pangburn Diner located across the street from the Taco Tackle Shack. When we moved her in lot #16 she wouldn't even let us buy her a new trailer home. So, we put her in my Me-Ma and Pa-Pa's trailer (My Pa-Pa had passed way three years earlier, and I had just put my Me-Ma in a nursin' home, so they weren't usin' their lot or their trailer). Dew's brother and sister, Darnell and Dottie, come up with their families from their homes in Texarkana to visit Momma Ballzak every Christmas. Me and my husband, Dew, take my momma, my daddy, and Momma Ballzak out to dinner every Sunday after church. And of course we take her into Searcy durin' the Christmas season so she can do her shoppin'. She still drives, but my husband, Dew, doesn't like her to drive out of the city limits on account of the time she got lost and ended up in Wichita Falls, Texas. She did meet a nice man durin' that trip named Juan, and she still writes to him every week. He even plans on comin' down and visitin' her just as soon as he gets out of prison in three to four years.

# LOT #17

Lot #17 is home to Mable (18) and Marty Scaggs (53). Mable moved in with Marty last November after a beautiful weddin' ceremony at the First Baptist Church of Pangburn. We were all happy to see Marty find someone as nice as Mable after the untimely passin' of his first wife, Eula, in October. They found Eula's lifeless body in the White River just a week after Marty reported her missin'. Accordin' to Sheriff Gentry, she must have been walkin' out by the river when she slipped, fell forward, accidentally puttin' her head into the plastic bag she was carryin', and fell into the river. It was a terrible freak accident. Of course nobody knows what Eula was doin' all the way over by White River. Her death was almost as surprisin' as Marty and Mable's engagement announcement. Who would have thought that Marty would have fallen in love with Mable? After all, she had been workin' at his construction company in Searcy as his secretary ever since she graduated from Pangburn High School. She had been under his nose for almost a year before his wife died, and they had never noticed each other in an emotional way. They spent their honeymoon floatin' down the White River, which had to be hard for poor old Marty seein' how the police had only found Eula's body there three weeks earlier.

# LOT #18

Me and my husband, Dew, live in lot #18. Seein' how I've already showed you our trailer, I thought I'd just move on. Now, I know many of y'all want to know our story. Well, I am currently workin' on my autobiography, which I hope to release some time in the future. I will tell y'all that me and my husband, Dew, have only been married for eleven years (we were late bloomers), but they've been the best eleven years anyone could ever have asked for. And I'll never forget the night he got down on his good knee and asked me to be his wife! Let me tell you, dear readers, nothin' says "I love you" like jewelry from Fingerhut. What could I say to a sexy man holdin' an adjustable faux diamond ring but "Yes." I'm proud to say neither one of us has ever regretted that moment durin' these past 10 years!

## LOT #19

Jeannie (52) and Jimmy Janssen (54) have the trailer in lot #19. There twin sons, Jack (37) and Josh (37) Janssen, were the boys that came up with the idea to blow up our septic tanks (see THE OFFICE). That was about the only good thing that them boys ever did. They were two holy terrors! They were always up to something evil. They used to steal my lawn statues and put 'em on top of my trailer. I finally had to hot-wire my little concrete creatures with a 220 charge just to keep those boys from touchin' 'em.

One night while Jeannie and Jimmy were at work, the boys took blue spray paint and painted the outside of their trailer home. Luckily Jeannie and Jimmy liked it because it would have cost an arm and a leg for them to restored it back to its original color. They also put a case of TIDY BOWL in the baptismal tank at the First Baptist Church of Pangburn. You can't imagine how mad Pastor Hickey was durin' that night's baptismal service. They went into the water a Caucasian person, and came back a freaky Smurf-like creature. Because of pranks like this, we were all surprised when the twins decided to become Baptist preachers! Jack pastors a large church in Jackson, Mississippi, with over 1,000 members, while his brother runs a 600-member church in Shreveport, Louisiana. Both boys also have church-related television shows that air in their states. They bring in enough money that Jeannie and Jimmy have been able to retire and even travel across the United States on the funds the twins send them each month.

## LOT #20

Lot #20 is the last lot in the High Chaparral Trailer Park and is home to Lovie (44) and Elmer Birch (48). Lovie and Elmer own the town newspaper, *The Pangburn Bugle*. Lovie is also our local Avon, Mary Kay, and Tupperware representative. So you can imagine all the hostessin' that she does in a month's time. I don't know how she does it! Elmer is a bigwig in the local Democratic Party, so durin' an election year, he and Lovie are always throwin' fund-raisin' gatherin's at their trailer. Of course, when Bill and Hilary came to town, bein' the close friends that they are with me and my husband, Dew, they stayed in our guest bedroom while Chelsea slept over at the Birch's trailer home. Lovie was not a happy camper! Pity!

# *Chapter 4*

Anita Biggon from lot #2 with a patron from her bar proudly shows off her **Devil in the Blue Dress Eggs**.

# *Appetizers*

The word *appetizer* is about as foreign in a trailer park as the word *monogamy*. They just aren't used! When we all sit down to eat, we sit down to eat! When it comes to trailer park vocabulary, the closest thing to an appetizer would probably be a "snack." Bein' the world traveler that I am, I know most people who live in homes without wheels consider a "snack" to be a light meal, which you might nibble on in between breakfast and lunch or lunch and dinner. This is not the case in our society! First off, we don't have lunch and dinner; we have dinner in the afternoon and supper in the evenin'. Second, we don't nibble, we eat, and trust me when I say you'll never hear the words *light* and *meal* used together in a trailer park. A snack in our community is somethin' you eat while you're preparin' dinner or supper, dustin', vacuumin', talkin' on the phone, or even while you're watchin' your soaps on TV. I guess you might say we're "appetizin'" all day long. What you will find is that these snack dishes are definitely not light in any sense of the word, but they sure are tasty. As a matter of fact, some of you folks might end up makin' a meal out of one of these dishes. If so, that's all right! It don't matter how you use 'em, just as long as you eat 'em. So feel free to use 'em as a snack, appetizer, or even as a covered dish for your next family, church, or school outin'. Just be prepared to get writer's cramp from the demand of request for the recipes!

# TRAILER TOAST

*This here is officially recognized nationwide as a
true trailer park dish.*

*Serves 4*

1 pound lean ground beef
1 onion
3 cups of milk
1/3 cup BISQUICK
1/4 teaspoon salt
1/4 teaspoon white pepper
12 pieces of toast

Brown hamburger and onion in a large skillet. Add BISQUICK, salt
and pepper, and mix well. Pour in milk and BISQUICK. Bring to a boil.
Cook for 5 minutes on high heat. Serve over toast.

—*JEANNIE JANSSEN, LOT #19*

# DEVIL IN THE BLUE DRESS EGGS

*Anita loves to pull a plate of these blue devils out
around closin' time at her bar just to play havoc
with some of her more drunk clientele.*

*Serves 8*

1 dozen hard-boiled eggs
1/2 cup French dressin'
1/2 teaspoon salt
1 teaspoon dry mustard
Some blue food colorin'

Shell eggs and cut in half lengthwise. Remove the yolk and mix with the
French dressin', salt, dry mustard, and enough food colorin' to make it a
bluish color. Replace the fillin' into the whites.

—*ANITA BIGGON, LOT #2*

# CHEESY CRACKERS

*Simple, but tasty.*

*Serves 4*

1 box of crackers

Government cheese

Lay crackers out on a plate. Slice Government cheese and place it on the crackers. Cook 'em in the microwave for 1 minute. Let 'em stand for 2 minutes. Eat!

—*LULU BELL BOXCAR, LOT #8*

# TRAILER MEAT SNACKS

*These little morsels pack a punch, let me tell you! So make sure you got plenty of water to drink when eatin' these things, 'cause you're gonna need it.*

*Serves 4*

1 can of SPAM, finely chopped

1/3 cup shredded Government cheese

1/4 cup finely chopped celery

1/4 cup mayonnaise

1 teaspoon hot pepper sauce

1 box of crackers

In bowl, combine all ingredients except crackers. Spread mixture on crackers. Place on bakin' sheet. Broil 1 minute or until cheese is melted.

—*JUANITA HIX, LOT #9*

# SASSY SALSA

*This here stuff is hotter than Houston in July.*

*Serves 4*

1 large can whole tomatoes

1 onion, chopped

1 bell pepper, chopped
1 clove garlic, chopped
1 can green chilies
1 can jalapenos, chopped
Salt
Pepper
Place in a blender and mix for 1 minute. Serve with chips.
—*DONNY OWENS, LOT #15*

## CALVARY CHEESE RAFTS

*By the time Sister Bertha has finished sayin' a blessin' over these rafts, they're usually cold, but still mighty tasty.*

*Serves 8–10*
25 slices white bread
Some melted margarine
8 oz. Government cheese
1 small onion, minced
2 tablespoons soft margarine
2 tablespoons prepared mustard

Cut each slice of bread in half and trim the crust off. Put crust aside for later. Toast the bread on one side. Brush untoasted sides with melted margarine.

Take bread crusts and cut each one in half. Place one piece of crust on cookie sheet. Take a tiny piece of cheese and put it on the middle of that piece of crust. Take another crust and place it across the first piece of crust makin' sure it rests on the tiny piece of cheese. The two pieces of crust should be in the shape of a cross. Place the 50 crust crosses in the oven and bake at 350 degrees until the cheese melts. Take out and let cool.

Combine remainin' cheese, onion, 2 tablespoons of margarine, and mustard. Mix well. Spread mixture onto buttered sides of bread. Broil until cheese melts. Plant a bread crust cross in the middle of the melted cheese. If it is at all possible, eat 'em while they're still warm.

—*SISTER BERTHA, LOT #12*

## HOT CHEESY BALLS

*My sister, Donna Sue, has always enjoyed rollin' balls in her hands.*

Serves 4–5

1 small jar of CHEEZ WIZ
1 lb. hot sausage
3 cups BISQUICK

Mix all in a large bowl. Add some beer if needed to roll in 1-inch balls. Place on ungreased cookie sheet. Bake 15 to 20 minutes at 400 degrees.

—*DONNA SUE BOXCAR, LOT #6*

## EL LOCCO LOG-O

*With or without the tequila, TUMS are required!*

Serves 4–10

3 oz. cream cheese
2 oz. shredded Government cheese
1 tablespoon lemon juice
1/4 teaspoon garlic salt
2 teaspoons chili powder
1 teaspoon paprika
1/2 cup finely chopped jalapeno peppers
1 cup tequila *(optional)*
1 cup crushed saltine crackers
1/2 cup green chili peppers

Let cheeses warm to room temperature. Put all ingredients in a bowl and mix together. Sprinkle extra paprika on wax paper. Place mixture on this and form into a log roll. Store in wax paper and chill. Slice into very thin slices, and serve on crackers.

—*LOIS BUNCH, LOT #3*

# EL DIABLO DIP-O

*After a few bites of this stuff, DO NOT try to operate heavy machinery!*

Serves 4

Use the same ingredients as the EL LOCCO LOG-O minus the cup of crackers. Add 2 more cups of tequila and mix well. Place in microwave for 4 minutes. Stir and cook for 2 more minutes. Serve with chips or just eat directly out of a bowl with a spoon.

—*ANITA BIGGON, LOT #2*

# TUNA TOWN WEDGES

*Tammy says she got this recipe from her cousin Tina Town in El Paso, Texas, two summers ago.*

Serves 4–8

3 hard-cooked eggs, chopped
7 oz. tuna, drained
4 oz. Government cheese
1/4 cup finely chopped bell pepper
1/4 cup finely chopped celery
2 tablespoons minced onion
1 tablespoon sweet pickle relish
1 tablespoon lemon juice
1/2 cup sour cream
1/2 stick of margarine, melted

1/2 teaspoon garlic salt

8 day-old hamburger buns

Combine margarine and garlic salt. Open the buns, and place the sliced sides up on a cookie sheet. Brush mixture on tops of bun slices and broil till lightly brown. Set aside.

Mix ingredients together, foldin' in sour cream. Spoon mixture onto each bun slice. Wrap each bun slice loosely in aluminum foil, making sure the foil doesn't touch the top of the mixture. Place the wrapped bun slice in the oven and bake for 30 to 35 minutes at 325 degrees. Take out of oven and unwrap. Cut each bun slice into four wedges.

*—TAMMY CANTRELL, LOT #1*

# DEMOCRATIC PARTY CHEESE SPREAD

*Lovie informs me that durin' LBJ's visits Lady Bird would always chase these down with Vodka Stingers.*

*Serves 4*

8 oz. cream cheese

1/2 cup shredded Government cheese

1/2 cup chopped nuts

1/4 cup milk

2 tablespoons snipped parsley

1/8 teaspoon onion powder

Let cream cheese and Government cheese get to room temperature. Mix everything together. Cover and chill for 24 hours. To serve, spread mixture on apple slices, crackers, celery sticks, or carrot sticks.

*—LOVIE BIRCH, LOT #20*

# OYSTERS ROCKEFELLER

*For some reason, a few of these after a night at the boy's trailer seems to turn my husband, Dew, into a wild animal when we get back home!*

*Serves 8*

2 cups chopped spinach (fresh)
1/4 cup finely chopped onion
24 oysters (in the shells)
3 tablespoons margarine, melted
2 tablespoons snipped parsley
1 clove garlic, minced
1/4 cup dry bread crumbs

Take a saucepan (pot) with a small amount of water in it and bring to a boil. Add spinach and onion, and let 'em cook for 3 minutes. Drain 'em and press out excess water.

Wash oysters thoroughly and then open the shells with a knife. Take out the oysters and let 'em dry. Throw away the top part of the shell, and clean the bottom part of the shell. Put the dry oysters back in the bottom part of the shell.

Mix together spinach, onion, 2 tablespoons of margarine, parsley, and garlic. Add a few drops of hot sauce if you like. Put a spoonful of mixture on top of each oyster.

Mix together bread crumbs and remainin' margarine. Sprinkle over the top of the mixture that is on the oysters. Take a bakin' pan and put crumpled foil in it so the oyster shells won't tip over. Put the oysters in the bakin' pan and bake at 425 degrees for 12 minutes.

—*KENNY LYNN, LOT #15*

—*DONNY OWENS, LOT #15*

# SWEET AND SOUR WIENIES

*If you're like me and love wienies, you'll love this recipe.*

*Serves 1–5 depending on how hungry you are*

1/2 cup pancake syrup

1/2 cup pineapple juice

3 tablespoons vinegar

2 tablespoons cornstarch

2 teaspoons Worcestershire sauce

1 teaspoon dry mustard

Package of wienies (cut each wienie into three pieces)

Stir everything but the wienies into a pot and place on the stove. Stir till it gets thick and starts to bubble. Add the wienies and cook for 8 minutes, stirrin' occasionally.

—*RUBY ANN BOXCAR, LOT # 18*

# OLLIE'S DILL DIP

*This will make you pucker up and whistle!*

*Serves 60 (6)*

40 lbs. cream cheese (8 oz.)

40 lbs. sour cream (8 oz.)

1 1/4 cups finely chopped green onions (2 tablespoons)

1/2 cup dried dillweed or dill pickle juice (2 teaspoons)

1/3 cup salt (1/2 teaspoon)

Mix together with an electric mixer softened cream cheese, sour cream, onion, dillweed, and salt until it is fluffy. Chill and serve with vegetable slices.

—*OLLIE WHITE, LOT #10*

## BATTER-FRIED VEGGIES

*Momma came up with this recipe in order to get*
*us kids to eat veggies*

*Serves 4*

1 egg

1 cup opened or fresh beer, cold (you can also use cold water or milk)

1 cup all-purpose flour

grease for deep fat fryin'

vegetables

Take egg and beat slightly, then mix in the beer. Add the flour all at once. Beat with a whisk till the mixture is smooth.

Take the veggies of your choice and cut into 2-inch slices (if you use onions, cut 'em like you would for onion rings). Make sure you pat the veggies dry.

Heat grease to 375 degrees. Dip the veggies into the batter, makin' sure that they're completely covered. Carefully place into the hot grease and cook for 2 to 3 minutes until lightly golden brown. Place the fried veggies on a paper towel and let 'em drain. Serve with thousand island dressin', ranch dressin', or your favorite dip. These are also great with soup.

*—MOMMA BOXCAR, LOT #5*

## SPAM'RACKERS

*Surprisin' enough, these ain't bad!*

*Makes 32 appetizers*

1 (7-ounce) can SPAM, finely cubed

1/3 cup shredded Government cheese

1/4 cup finely chopped celery

1/4 cup MIRACLE WHIP

1 tablespoon chopped parsley

1/8 teaspoon hot pepper sauce

Crackers

In bowl, combine all ingredients except crackers. Spread mixture on crackers. Place on bakin' sheet. Broil 1 to 2 minutes or until cheese is melted.

*—LULU BELL BOXCAR, LOT #8*

# BROCCOLI TEMPTATIONS

*I've cooked these at home and they're wonderful,*
*but Juanita tends to overcook the broccoli and it*
*always comes out tough and hard, God bless her.*

Serves 4

2 packages broccoli stems and pieces (if frozen, thaw before cooking)

1 medium onion, chopped

1 can cream of mushroom soup

3/4 cup MIRACLE WHIP

2 hard-boiled eggs

4 cups Government cheese (VELVEETA is great, too), shredded

3 cups crackers, crushed

3 tablespoons margarine

Cut up the onion. Boil the broccoli and onion together until cooked. In a large bowl, mix soup, MIRACLE WHIP, eggs, and half the cheese. Add cooked broccoli and onion, and stir well. Pour mixture into a greased casserole dish. Cover with the rest of the cheese and the crushed crackers. Top with margarine. Bake in a 350 degree oven for 35 minutes.

*—JUANITA HIX, LOT #9*

# THE KATHY LEE GIFFORD TRIBUTE CHEESE DIP

*Lulu Bell came up with this dish while watchin'
one of Kathy Lee's Christmas specials.*

*Serves 6*
24 oz. cream cheese
1 can tomato soup
1/2 cup water
1 package lemon JELL-O
1/2 cup pecans, finely chopped
1/2 cup onion, finely chopped
1/2 cup bell pepper, finely chopped

Dissolve the JELL-O in the water and pour it into a pot along with the cream cheese and soup. Put over medium heat and cook, stirring occasionally, until the cream cheese melts.

In a large bowl, put all the finely chopped ingredients and mix thoroughly. Pour the melted mixture over the finely chopped mixture. Mix well and put it in the fridge for 3 hours or until the cheese has hardened again. Serve with crackers or chips.

—*LULU BELL BOXCAR, LOT #8*

# LOIS'S CHILI CON QUESO

*I always have to watch how much of this I eat
'cause it tends to give me diarrhea if I don't.*

*Serves 6*
2.5 lbs. Government cheese, grated
13 oz. water
3/4 cup onion, chopped
1/2 cup celery
1/2 cup green bell pepper
1/8 cup jalapeno pepper, chopped

Take a double boiler and combine the cheese and 3 cups of water. Bring it to a boil, stirrin' every so often until the cheese has melted.

Combine the onion, celery, bell pepper, and jalapenos in a pot. Add 1/4 cup of water and cook over medium heat until it starts to boil. Remove from heat and mix with the melted cheese. Serve with chips.

*—LOIS BUNCH, LOT #3*

# *Chapter 5*

Tammy Cantrell of lot #1 holdin' a pitcher of her
**Homemade Grape Soda Pop.**

# *Beverages*

Everybody that lives in a trailer park loves beverages, and to tell the truth, I really don't know why. Obviously it's not because we've done anything to work up a thirst. That's for damn sure. But you can walk into any trailer home in America and every one of the occupants will have a beverage near 'em. Maybe it all goes back to the days when trailers didn't have air-conditionin' units in 'em. Back then everybody had a box fan in every window of the trailer. Or perhaps it stems from a way of showin' you got money. Sure your car is out in your driveway up on cinder blocks, but hey, you can still afford a refreshin' beverage whenever you feel like it. Or possibly it's simply a "just in case." Just in case the air breaks down I've got a beverage to beat the heat. Or just in case my legs fall asleep while I'm watchin' TV, and I get thirsty, I've got a beverage close by. Or just in case I drop my cigarette down the couch, I can pour some of my beverage in there to put it out. Regardless of what the reason might be, everybody that lives in a trailer home has a beverage in their hands at all time.

You'll also find that the beverage containers ain't your normal size either. Oh, no, we got those great big 60-ounce cups that we fill to the top with ice and then add our favorite beverages. This is in case we get talkin' on the phone or watchin' somethin' on TV and don't want to have to get up to refill our glasses.

# COCOA MIX

*This stuff is better than the kind you find at the
Piggly Wiggly.*

Serves 45

10 cups powdered milk

4 3/4 cups powdered sugar

2 cups finely crushed COCOA PUFFS

1 3/4 cups powdered nondairy creamer

Combine all together until thoroughly mixed. Store mixture in empty coffee cans or any airtight container.

When you're ready to make a cup, place 1/3 cup of the mixture in a coffee cup. Add hot water and stir until the mixture dissolves. Serve with marshmallows or whipped cream if you like.

—*OLLIE WHITE, LOT #10*

# MOMMA BALLZAK'S GRAPE APE

*These sure are great when you're BBQin', but
don't make the same mistake we did. Keep these
drinks away from the grill!*

Makes one drink

Juice of 1/2 lime

2 oz. gin

Chilled grape juice

Fill a tall glass halfway with crushed ice and add the lime juice. Carefully add the gin and chilled grape juice to the glass. Stir and then garnish with a lime wedge.

—*MOMMA BALLZAK, LOT #16*

# MOMMA BALLZAK'S GRAPE APE'S UGLY SISTER

*If anyone other than Momma Ballzak had come
up with this adult beverage, I'd have said they
had a drinkin' problem.*

*Makes one drink*
Juice of 1/2 lime
2 oz. whisky
Chilled grape juice
Fill a tall glass halfway with crushed ice and add the lime juice. Carefully add the whisky and chilled grape juice to the glass. Stir and then garnish with a lime wedge.

*—MOMMA BALLZAK, LOT #16*

## WANDA'S WILD PEANUT BUTTER CHOCOLATE COOKIES DRINK

*This drink is great for both kids and adults.*

*Serves 2 (8 oz. glasses)*
1 pint chocolate or vanilla ice cream
3 peanut butter cups, broken up
5 chocolate wafer cream-filled cookies (recipe is in COOKIE section)
1 teaspoon imitation vanilla extract
1/2 cup milk
2 tablespoons peanut butter
Put ice cream, peanut butter cups, 3 chocolate wafer cream-filled cookies, imitation vanilla extract, milk, and peanut butter into a blender. Blend until the cookies are coarsely chopped. Pour into glasses and top off with a whole chocolate wafer cream-filled cookie.

*—WANDA KAY, LOT #13*

## HOMEMADE GRAPE SODA POP

*If you like the store-bought grape soda, then this stuff will make you dance!*

*Makes 2 liters*
8 6-ounce cans of frozen grape juice concentrate
Carbonated water

Empty out two of the grape juice cans into a quart pitcher. Take each can and fill it up with carbonated water three times per can. Stir until well mixed. Take a funnel and pour the drink into an old empty rinsed out 2-liter soda pop bottle. Continue makin' the grape juice and carbonated mix until the 2-liter bottle is full. Put soda pop bottle lid on tight. Serve over ice.

You can make other flavored soda pops by simply usin' your favorite juice concentrate in place of the grape.

—*TAMMY CANTRELL, LOT #1*

## SODA POPPERS

*These are great, but be careful when placin' the trays in the freezer or you'll end up with a sticky mess.*

*Makes 14 cubes dependin' on your ice tray size*

Take an ice tray and fill each ice slot with your favorite soda pop. Put in freezer and let it freeze. When you're ready to have a glass of soda pop, use these SODA POPPERS in place of ice cubes.

—*NELLIE TINKLE, LOT #4*

## JUICE POPPERS

*When I've got to drive my Me-Ma anywhere I always place a few of these in a cup so the old lady has somethin' to suck on.*

*Makes 14 cubes dependin' on your ice tray size*

Take an ice tray and fill each ice slot with your favorite fruit juices. Put in freezer and let it freeze. When you're ready to have a glass of fruit juice, use these JUICE POPPERS in place of ice cubes.

—*NELLIE TINKLE, LOT #4*

# DR PEPPER EGGNOG

*My husband, Dew, just loves this at Christmas-*
*time.*

*Serves 12 (4-oz. glasses)*

4 eggs

4 tablespoons powdered sugar

4 tablespoons rum

3 cups milk

1/2 teaspoon imitation vanilla extract

2 cans cold DR PEPPER

Beat the egg whites to a dry froth. Beat into the egg whites the powdered sugar, and then the egg yolks, rum, and imitation vanilla extract. Add the milk and stir. Pour the DR PEPPER into mixture and serve. To keep the eggnog cold for a long period of time, add Nellie Tinkle's DR PEPPER flavored SODA POPPERS.

*—CONNIE KAY, LOT #13*

# DR PEPPER PUNCH

*Connie always whips up a batch of this for my*
*husband's birthday.*

*Makes 1 punch bowl*

1 liter DR PEPPER

1 48-oz. can pineapple juice, chilled

1 quart pineapple sherbet

Combine all together just before servin'. To keep the punch cold for a long period of time, add Nellie Tinkle's DR PEPPER–flavored SODA POPPERS or her pineapple JUICE POPPERS.

*—CONNIE KAY, LOT #13*

# PIT BULL PUNCH

*Trust me when I say don't serve this to the elderly,*
*'cause they tend to get real mean and hateful!*

*Makes 1 punch bowl*

1/2 cup rum
1 cup sugar
2 cups water
1 gallon MAD DOG 20/20
1 orange
1 lemon
2 limes

Wash fruit thoroughly, and cut it into slices. Put the water and the fruit in a blender. Blend for 2 minutes. Pour the blended contents into a punch bowl. Add the rest of the ingredients and stir well. Put all breakables in a safe place.

—*KYLE CHITWOOD, LOT #11*

# TRAILER PARK TEA

*This beats the heat durin' the summertime.*

*Makes 1 gallon*

1 package Cherry JELL-O (dissolve in 2 cups water)
1 large can pineapple juice
2 sticks cinnamon
15 cloves
2 tablespoons lemon juice
1 gallon tea bag

Add all the ingredients together and brew. Steep for 20 minutes. Add one cup of sugar and enough water to make a gallon batch. Heat and serve or pour over ice.

—*DOTTIE LAMB, LOT #14*

## EULA'S PERCOLATOR PUNCH

*Marty and Mable served this at their weddin' in Eula's honor. There wasn't a dry eye at the reception.*

*Makes about 1 1/2 quarts*

2 cups cranberry juice

2 cups pineapple juice

1/3 cup brown sugar

1 cup water

1 tablespoon whole cloves

2 sticks cinnamon (broken up)

Dissolve sugar in water. Pour juices and sugar-water mixture in percolator. Place cloves and cinnamon in the basket where you would normally put the ground coffee. Perk through cycle.

—*MABLE SKAGGS, LOT #17*

## MOMMA BALLZAK'S ICED TEA

*If you're drinkin' this at a neighbors home, plan on stayin' the night!*

*Makes about a gallon*

2 liters vodka

1 liter 7 UP

1 gallon tea bag

Mix together the vodka and 7 UP in a gallon pitcher. Put the tea bag in. Twenty minutes later take the tea bag out and throw it in the trash. Make sure none of your pets can get to the tea bag. Pour over ice, and sit back to watch TV.

—*MOMMA BALLZAK, LOT #16*

# Chapter 6

Kitty and Kyle Chitwood of lot #11 display their
**Low Life Bar Fly Biscuits**.

# *Breads*

Breads are a vital part of any trailer park meal. After all, if you didn't have bread, what would you use to sop up your gravy with? Plus bread is a great ingredient to add when you need to stretch a meal. Hell, look at meatloaf! Breads are also a great way to get your guest halfway full, thus leavin' more of the main dish for you to eat. In the trailer park community, the normal bread is always white; however more and more people are tryin' new types of bread. So don't worry if white bread ain't your favorite, because there are several different types of bread recipes in this section. We even have some breads that don't require any yeast to make 'em. Regardless what kind of bread you make, there are two items you will also need, a knife and some butter. And remember to cut the bread on top of somethin', 'cause the counter-top material that you'll find in every trailer will scratch if you just look at it.

## BANANA NUT BREAD

*This is some good eatin'!*

*Makes one loaf*

2 2/3 cups regular flour
3 teaspoons bakin' powder
1 teaspoon salt
1/2 teaspoon bakin' soda
1 stick margarine
1 cup sugar
3 eggs

2 medium ripe bananas, peeled and mashed

3/4 cup chopped pecans

Grease a loaf pan (9 × 5 × 3), and line bottom with wax paper. Sift flour, bakin' powder, salt, and soda together. Cream margarine with sugar until fluffy. Beat in eggs, one at a time, until fluffy again. Stir in flour mixture alternately with mashed bananas. Fold in pecans. Pour into prepared pan and bake at 325 degrees for 2 hours and 20 minutes. After completely cool, wrap and store over night for easier slicing.

—*DORA DYKEMAN, LOT #7*

## HONKEY TONKIN' HUSBAND BREAD

*You don't have to be married to enjoy this stuff.*

*Makes 1 loaf*

3 cups self-risin' flour

5 tablespoons sugar

12 oz. can of beer that's been left open overnight at room temperature

Mix all together and place into a well-greased loaf pan. Bake for 50 minutes at 350 degrees.

—*KITTY CHITWOOD, LOT #11*

## LOW LIFE BAR FLY BISCUITS

*Also known in northern Arkansas as*
*DONNA SUE ROLLS.*

*Makes 16 biscuits if you portion 'em out just right*

Same ingredients as used for HONKEY TONKIN' HUSBAND BREAD.

Take batter and roll into 1-inch balls. Place the balls on a well-greased pan, and slightly flatten them. Cook at 350 degrees until golden brown.

—*KITTY CHITWOOD, LOT #11*

# SLUT PUPPIES

*If you got any of these left over after a meal, save
'em. You can spray paint 'em and hang 'em on
your Christmas tree durin' the holiday season.*

*Serves 4*

1 cup corn meal
1 cup flour
1/3 cup sugar
4 teaspoons bakin' powder
1 onion, chopped
1 cup of beer that's been left open overnight at room temperature

Mix well, shape into 1-inch balls, and drop into deep grease until
brown. Drain on paper towel.

*—KITTY CHITWOOD, LOT #11*

# OLLIE'S AWARD-WINNING CORN BREAD

*There ain't nothin' like Ollie's cornbread and a
big tub of margarine!*

*Makes 10 skillets (1 skillet)*

1 and 1/4 gallons buttermilk (2 cups)
1 and 1/4 gallons corn meal (2 cups)
10 eggs (1 egg)
1/4 cup bakin' soda (1 teaspoon)
1/4 cup salt (1 teaspoon)

Mix well and put in a skillet (or 9-inch pan) that has been heated with
oil in it. Bake at 375 to 400 degrees for about 20 minutes or until nicely
brown.

*—OLLIE WHITE, LOT #10*

## COCOA BREAD (HOME RECIPE)

*I love to put a big slice of this in a bowl with ice cream and some chocolate syrup.*

*Makes 1 loaf*

1/4 cup finely ground COCOA PUFFS
1/4 cup sugar
1/2 teaspoon salt
1 cup milk
3 tablespoons shortenin'
1 yeast cake
1/4 cup lukewarm water
3 1/2 cups flour

Mix the COCOA PUFFS, sugar, and salt. Add the milk, which has been scalded, and the shortenin'. Let stand until lukewarm and add the yeast, which has been softened in the lukewarm water. Add enough flour to make a dough that can be handled and knead until smooth and elastic. Let rise until doubled in bulk. Bake 1 hour at 350 degrees.

—*OLLIE WHITE, LOT #10*

## ZUCCHINI NUT BREAD

*This usually goes real fast at all the covered-dish functions at the First Baptist Church of Pangburn.*

*Makes 1 loaf*

4 eggs
1 1/2 cups brown sugar, packed
3/4 cup vegetable oil
3 cups unsifted unbleached flour
1 1/2 teaspoons bakin' soda
3/4 teaspoon bakin' powder
3/4 teaspoon salt

2 teaspoons cinnamon

2 cups grated zucchini, unpeeled

1 cup coarsely chopped nuts

1 teaspoon imitation vanilla extract

Beat eggs well; gradually beat in sugar, and then oil. Combine dry ingredients. Add to egg mixture alternately with zucchini. Stir in nuts and vanilla. Turn into greased and floured 9-inch pan. Bake at 350 degrees for 50 minutes. Remove from oven and let set 10 minutes. Turn out and cool.

*—NELLIE TINKLE, LOT #4*

# DIVINE DOUGHNUTS

*These will make you thank God for taste buds!*

*Makes just enough*

2 eggs

1 cup sugar

1 tablespoon vinegar

1 tablespoon nutmeg

1/2 teaspoon salt

1 cup milk

3 cups flour

3 heapin' teaspoons bakin' powder

Beat eggs, add sugar, vinegar, nutmeg, and salt. Beat well, addin' milk alternately with flour and bakin' powder. Knead well until firm. Roll on floured board, 1/3 inch thick; cut with doughnut cutter or glass (if you use the glass make sure to use a thimble to cut out the doughnut hole). Heat 1 1/2 inches of grease or cookin' oil in pan and fry a few at a time until golden brown. Drain on a paper towel. Ice doughnuts and holes with CHRISTIAN CREAM CHEESE FROSTIN'.

*—SISTER BERTHA, LOT #12*

## CHRISTIAN CREAM CHEESE FROSTIN'

*I'll make up a bowl of this frostin' and eat it by itself.*

Makes enough for doughnuts or cake

1/2 cup margarine

4 oz. cream cheese

1/2 box powdered sugar

1 teaspoon imitation vanilla extract

Mix all ingredients well and spread on cooled doughnuts, doughnut holes, or cake.

—*SISTER BERTHA, LOT #12*

## SPAMCAKES AND SYRUP

*These are actually great tastin'.*

Serves 4

1 1/2 cups pancake mix

1 cup milk

8 oz. can cream-style corn

1 egg

1 tablespoon cookin' oil

7 oz. can SPAM, finely chopped

Combine pancake mix, milk, corn, egg, and oil. Stir in SPAM. Pour 1/3 cup of batter on greased fryin' pan and cook over medium heat until browned on bottom. Turn and brown other side. Serve with maple syrup.

—*MOMMA BALLZAK, LOT #16*

## TRAILER PARK SWEET MUFFINS

*The Janssen twins used to swipe these from the dinner table and drop 'em off the bridge over the highway at passin' cars.*

*Makes 18 large muffins*
1 egg
1/4 cup oil
1/2 cup milk
1 1/2 cups flour
1/2 cup sugar
2 teaspoons bakin' powder
1/2 teaspoon salt

Grease muffin pans. Beat egg, stir in oil and milk. Mix in remainin' ingredients. Fill muffin pan to 2/3 full. Bake at 400 degrees for 20 to 25 minutes.

*—JEANNIE JANSSEN, LOT #19*

## PEANUT BUTTER MUFFINS

*I love to dip these in hot fudge!*

*Makes 18 large muffins*
1/2 cup brown sugar, packed
1/4 cup margarine
1/2 cup peanut butter
2 eggs
1 cup sifted white flour
1 cup sifted whole wheat flour
3 teaspoons bakin' powder
1/4 teaspoon salt
1 1/4 cups milk

Blend sugar and margarine. Add peanut butter and mix until creamy. Add eggs and beat until smooth. Sift flours, bakin' powder, and salt together, and add alternately with the milk. Begin and end with the flour. Mix well. Bake in greased muffin tins at 400 degrees for 12 to 15 minutes.

*—OPAL LAMB, LOT #14*

## DONNA SUE'S SPAM MUFFINS

*My sister serves these to all her one-night-stands
for breakfast the next mornin'. If you're wonder-
ing how they taste, just remember thousands of
uneducated gutter trash scum of the earth can't
be wrong!*

*Makes 12 muffins*
4 tablespoons shortenin'
1 cup chopped SPAM
1 egg
1 cup graham flour
1 cup white flour
3 teaspoons bakin' powder
1 cup milk

Cream shortenin' and add SPAM. Add egg, beat well, and then add the
dry ingredients, mixed and sifted, alternately with the milk. Mix well and
put into greased muffin pans. Bake in a 400-degree oven for 30 minutes.
—*DONNA SUE BOXCAR, LOT #6*

## SPAM AND CHEESE MUFFIN ROLLS

*When I was a little girl, my momma would use a
hot fresh batch of these to get me out of bed on
Sunday mornin's for church.*

*Serves 4*
1-pound loaf frozen bread dough, thawed
3 tablespoons prepared mustard
1 tablespoon honey
2 cups Government cheese, shredded
7 oz. SPAM, thinly sliced

On floured surface, roll dough into 21 × 12-inch rectangle. In small
bowl, combine mustard and honey. Spread mustard mixture over dough.
Sprinkle dough with cheese. Lay SPAM slices over cheese. Startin' with

long side, roll dough up tightly. Cut dough into 12 equal slices. Place slices, cut sides up, in greased muffin cups, pressin' slightly. Cover. Let rise in warm place 45 minutes or until doubled in size. Heat oven to 375 degrees. Bake 30 minutes or until golden brown. Cover with foil halfway through bakin' if rolls are becomin' too dark.

*—MOMMA BOXCAR, LOT #5*

## SOPAIPILLAS

*These will melt in your mouth!*

*Makes 6 to 12*

2 cups flour
2 teaspoons bakin' powder
1 teaspoon salt
1 egg
3 tablespoons vegetable oil
1/2 cup water

Stir together well and roll out on bread board. Heat vegetable oil to 380 degrees. Drop rolled and thin-cut triangles into oil. Deep fry for 3 to 4 minutes. Drain on paper towel and serve with honey.

*—LOIS BUNCH, LOT #3*

## SINNIN' MAN ROLLS

*These will make you forget your husband didn't come home last night! Of course, us happily married gals can eat these also.*

*Makes 18 to 36 rolls dependin' on how you slice them*

1 cup lukewarm water
2 cups warm milk
1 egg, beaten
2 tablespoons sugar
1/2 cup and 2 tablespoons oil

5 1/4 cups all-purpose flour
1 package dry yeast
2 tablespoons margarine, melted
2 teaspoons salt
1/4 cup of HOT DAMN
4 teaspoons sugar
4 teaspoons ground cinnamon
Combine water and milk; add yeast, stirrin' until dissolved. Add egg, 2
teaspoons of sugar, oil, and 2 1/4 cups flour. Cover and let rise in a warm
place for 2 hours. Stir in salt and remainin' flour. Let dough rest a few minutes. Roll out dough to 1/4-inch thickness. Combine melted margarine
and HOT DAMN, and then brush it on the dough. Combine 4 teaspoons
sugar and ground cinnamon, and sprinkle on the dough. Roll up jelly-roll
fashion, beginnin' at the long side. Seal edges. Cut into 1/2-inch slices and
place in greased round pan. Cover and let rise in a warm place until doubled in bulk, or 35 minutes. Bake at 350 degrees for 20 minutes.

*—KITTY CHITWOOD, LOT #11*

# SPAM ROLL

*The kids at the school just love these rolls.*

*Serves 50 (3–4)*
10 12-oz. cans SPAM, ground up (one 12 oz. can)
2 quarts and 1 pint sour cream (1cup)
1 quart and 1/2 pint peas (1/2 cup)
1 gallon and 1 quart BISQUICK (2 cups)
1 1/4 cups crumbled dehydrated onion flakes (2 teaspoons)
1/2 gallon and 10 oz. milk (1/2 cup plus 2 tablespoons)
*BELOW IS THE CUT-DOWN RECIPE*
Stir together SPAM, 1/3 cup sour cream and peas, and set aside. Combine BISQUICK and onion flakes; add 1/2 cup milk. Stir just until the
dough forms into a ball. Roll it out on a lightly floured surface until it
makes a 12 × 9-inch rectangle; spread with "SPAM" mixture. Roll it up

jelly-roll fashion, beginnin' at long end; pinch dough together to seal. Place on a greased bakin' sheet, seam side down; brush with 1 tablespoon milk. Bake in 400-degree oven about 25 minutes, or until browned.

While it's cookin', combine remainin' sour cream and 1 tablespoon milk. Cut roll into slices to serve. Put the sour cream and milk mixture on top of each slice.

*—OLLIE WHITE, LOT #10*

## ME-MA'S HOT BREAD

*We're gettin' her help!*

*Makes 12*

12 slices bread

1 bottle hot salsa

Melted margarine

Spread margarine on one side of bread. Broil until golden brown. Pour salsa on each slice. Serve. Dogs love it as treats, and makes great Christmas gifts when wrapped festively.

*—ME-MA, FORMERLY OF LOT #8*

## HANK WILLIAMS, JR. BREAD

*Anita named this loaf after one of her favorite loafs.*

*Makes 1 loaf*

2 loaves frozen bread dough (like you find in the freezer section)

1 can cold unopened beer

1 small bag pretzels

1 can beer nuts

8 oz. Government cheese

1 can SPAM

Thaw out bread loaves. Take a loaf and spread it out on a greased cookie sheet. Leave a little dough on all four sides.

Smash the pretzels into bite-size pieces and pour into a bowl. Add the beer nuts and cheese. Cut the SPAM into small cubes. Add the SPAM cubes and 1/4 cup of beer into the bowl with the other ingredients. Mix well, and spread onto the dough.

Take the second loaf and spread it on top of the mixture and first loaf. Pinch the two loafs together along the sides, sealin' the ends. Brush margarine on the top and bake for 50 minutes at 350 degrees. Drink the rest of the beer while you wait on the bread to cook.

*—ANITA BIGGON, LOT #2*

## SPAM IN THE HOLE ROLLS

*This is a twist on a recipe I got from my dear friend the Queen, durin' one of my many trips to London. After a bite of these reconfigured rolls, Liz gave 'em her royal seal of approval!*

*Makes 16*

12 oz. can SPAM, cut into small pieces
1/2 cup chopped onion
6 oz. can tomato paste
4 oz. can sliced mushrooms, drained
3/4 cup shredded Government cheese
2 cans store-bought crescent roll dough

Separate dough into 16 triangles. Combine all the other ingredients. Mix well and spoon mixture onto the triangles at the wide end. Roll the triangles up. Place on bakin' sheet. Bake at 375 degrees for 15 to 20 minutes or until golden brown.

*—RUBY ANN BOXCAR, LOT #18*

# RISE AND SHINE, AND GIVE GOD
# THE GLORY BISCUITS

*Just another good reason to be a Baptist.*

*Makes 16*
4 cups self-risin' flour
1 tablespoon sugar
1 tablespoon bakin' powder
2 cups buttermilk
2/3 cup shortenin'

Mix all the ingredients together. DON'T KNEAD the dough! Roll it out to a 1-inch thickness, and brush the top of the dough with a little extra buttermilk. Cut out a desired-size biscuit and place on a greased bakin' sheet. Cook at 400 degrees for 15 minutes. Serve with butter and grape jelly.

*—SISTER BERTHA, LOT #12*

# Chapter 7

Outside of their department store stand Opal and Dottie Lamb
of lot #14 with their **Lemon Cheesecake**.

# Cakes

We trailer folks stand by the sayin', "Cakes ain't just for birthdays any more." There doesn't have to be any kind of special celebration for us to pop one in the oven. Hell, if you wake up breathin' then you might as well make a cake. As you might have guessed by my introduction, we will throw just about anything in a cake. It doesn't matter, because after years of experimentin' we've been able to make just about anything taste good in cake form. The only rules that we have when it comes to eatin' cake are listed below.

1. Don't take more than you can eat.
2. Whoever finds the longest piece of hair in their cake has to clean all the dishes that night (this is to insure no one complains about your terrible hair loss condition).
3. Whoever eats the last piece of cake has to kiss the cook (this is to insure the cook gets the last piece of cake).
4. If your Grandma or Grandpa fall asleep while eatin' cake, whatever's left on their plates is fair game just as long as they don't wake up.

*All recipes make one cake with the exception of some of Ollie White's recipes.*

## DONNA SUE'S DAY-OLD DELIGHT CAKE

*This cake is best when served one day after makin' it.*

1 box yellow cake mix
8 oz. cream cheese
1 package instant vanilla puddin'

75

2 cups milk, cold
1 large can crushed pineapple, drained
1 tub whipped cream
Nuts (optional)
Coconut (optional)

Bake the cake accordin' to the box. Let it cool for 20 minutes before preparin' the followin' toppin'. Beat the cream cheese until it's fluffy. Make the puddin' usin' the 2 cups of cold milk. Add the puddin' to the cream cheese, and let it stand until it thickens. Spread it on the cake. Carefully spread the pineapple on top. Apply the whipped cream. Sprinkle on nuts and coconut if desired. Let the cake stand overnight in the fridge.

—*DONNA SUE BOXCAR, LOT #6*

# APPLESAUCE CAKE

*This is one of Ollie's best creations. It's so moist
and tender, it almost beats sex. Almost!*

2 1/2 quarts margarine (1 cup)
1 gallon and 1 quart sugar (2 cups)
1/4 cup imitation vanilla extract (1 teaspoon)
1 gallon and 1 quart applesauce (2 cups)
2 1/2 quarts raisins (1 cup)
2 1/2 quarts pecans, broken (1 cup)
5 lbs. flour (3 cups)
1/4 cup cinnamon (1 teaspoon)
1/4 cup nutmeg (1 teaspoon)
2/3 cup bakin' soda (1 and 3/4 teaspoons)
2 tablespoons salt (1/4 teaspoon)

*BELOW IS THE CUT-DOWN RECIPE*

Cream margarine and sugar until light and fluffy. Add vanilla, applesauce, raisins, and pecans that have been dredged in 1/4 cup of the flour. Sift all dry ingredients, includin' the remainin' flour, together and add to mixture. Pour into a loaf pan and bake at 325 degrees for 2 hours. This cake keeps indefinitely and gets better with time. You can eat plain or top with a creamy CARAMEL ICIN'.

—*OLLIE WHITE, LOT #10*

## EULA'S BANANA SPLIT CAKE

*Every time I'd get back into town from one of my singin' engagements, Eula would make one of these and bring it over. I sure do miss that old gal.*

*CRUST:*
2 cups vanilla wafers, finely crushed
3/4 cubes melted margarine
*FILLIN':*
2 cups powdered sugar
2 egg whites
1/2 cup margarine, softened
1 teaspoon imitation vanilla extract
*TOPPIN'S:*
15 oz. can crushed pineapple, drained
6 bananas, sliced
1 box of instant banana pie fillin'
2 cartons whipped cream
Nuts
Maraschino cherries

Combine crust ingredients and pat into an ungreased 9 × 13-inch pan. Then cream together all of the fillin' ingredients in a bowl until fluffy. Spread fillin' over crust. Put the toppin' fruits on top of the fillin'. Pour the banana pie fillin' on the top of the fruit. Add the whipped cream and then nuts. Top it off with cherries. Cool it for one hour. Store in the fridge.

—*MABLE SKAGGS, LOT #17*

## SOUR CREAM BANANA CAKE

*This is like an orgasm for your mouth! If any of you gals ain't had an orgasm, then this is as close to it as you can get.*

1/4 cup margarine
1 1/3 cups sugar
2 eggs
1 teaspoon imitation vanilla extract
2 cups sifted flour
1 teaspoon bakin' soda
1 teaspoon bakin' powder
3/4 teaspoon salt
1 cup sour cream
1 cup ripe bananas, smashed
1/2 cup chopped nuts

Cream margarine and sugar. Add eggs and vanilla. Blend well. Sift the next four ingredients together, and add alternately with sour cream to the egg mixture. Add bananas and nuts. Mix well. Pour into a greased 13 × 9 × 2-inch pan and bake at 350 degrees for 45 minutes. Serve plain or with a RUBY ANN'S FROSTIN'.

*—JUANITA HIX, LOT #9*

## BUTTERMILK CAKE

*After a bite of this you'll know how Tammy got her hips.*

2 sticks margarine, softened
2 cups sugar
4 eggs
1 teaspoon lemon extract
3 cups flour
1/2 teaspoon salt

1/2 teaspoon bakin' powder

1/2 teaspoon bakin' soda

1 cup buttermilk

Put the first four ingredients in a bowl and beat for 2 1/2 minutes. Add the remaining ingredients and beat for another 2 1/2 minutes. Pour into a loaf or tube pan and bake for 1 hour at 350 degrees. Serve plain or with BUTTERMILK ICIN'.

*—TAMMY CANTRELL, LOT #1*

## TRAILER PARK CHEESECAKE

*Nellie will fix up one of these and bring it down to the Great Big Balls Bowlin' Alley when our church league bowls. I can't tell you what it does for our morale.*

1 package lemon JELL-O

1 cup boilin' water

3 tablespoons lemon juice

8 oz. cream cheese

1 cup sugar

1 teaspoon imitation vanilla extract

1 can chilled sweetened condensed milk, whipped (recipe's in the COOKIE section)

1 lb. graham crackers

1/2 cup margarine

Dissolve JELL-O in boilin' water, and add lemon juice. Let it cool.

Cream together cheese, sugar, and vanilla. Add JELL-O mixture, and mix well. Fold whipped milk into mixture.

Crush graham crackers into very fine crumbs and add melted margarine. Firmly pack 2/3 of the crumbs into a 9 × 13 × 2-inch pan, coverin' both bottom and sides. Add fillin' and sprinkle remainin' graham crackers on top. Chill for several hours. Cut into squares and serve.

*—NELLIE TINKLE, LOT #4*

# LEMON CHEESECAKE

*Dottie has got some kind of infatuation with lemons, but that's all right just as long as the lemon dishes she makes taste as good as this one. After a visit to Neiman Marcus, Dottie came back, installed a little cooler in the store, and started sellin' food items like this one. When I go in to buy my husband, Dew, a pair of pants I also treat myself to a slice of her cheesecake.*

3 oz. package lemon-flavored gelatin

1 cup boilin' water

3 teaspoons lemon juice

8 oz. package cream cheese

1 cup sugar

1 teaspoon imitation vanilla extract

13 oz. sweetened condensed milk, whipped (recipe's in the COOKIE section)

3 cups graham cracker crumbs

1/2 cup margarine, melted

Dissolve gelatin in the boilin' water. Add lemon juice and cool. Cream together cheese, sugar, and imitation vanilla extract. Add gelatin and mix well. Fold whipped milk into gelatin mixture.

Crush graham crackers into fine crumbs and add melted margarine. Firmly pack 2/3 of mixture in bottom and sides of 9 × 11 × 2-inch pan. Add fillin' and spread with spatula. Sprinkle remainin' cracker crumbs over top.

*—DOTTIE LAMB, LOT #14*

# WANDA'S COTTAGE CHEESE CAKE

*This is not my Me-Ma's recipe so don't let the name scare you! It tastes just fine.*

1 1/2 cups cottage cheese
1 egg, separated
1 package gelatin (envelope)
1/8 teaspoon salt
1 cup sugar
1 cup milk, divided in half
1 tablespoon lemon juice
1 teaspoon imitation vanilla extract
6 tablespoons whipped cream

Put cottage cheese and half of the milk in a blender and blend until it's smooth.

Put egg yolk in the top of a double boiler and beat well. Add remaining milk, gelatin, and salt. Cook, stirrin', over boilin' water for 10 minutes or until the gelatin dissolves. Remove from the heat and add the sugar. Let it cool. Add the cottage cheese/milk mixture, lemon juice, and imitation vanilla extract. Chill, stirrin' occasionally, until the mixture mounds when dropped from a spoon. Beat the egg white until it stiffens. Fold the egg white and whipped cream together into the mixture. Pour it into a graham cracker crust and let chill for an hour.

*—WANDA KAY, LOT #13*

# CHEESE SPAM CAKE

*Personally, I have served this as a meat dish at several **Tupperware** parties I've hosted.*

FILLING:
16 oz. garden vegetable flavored cream cheese
3 eggs
1 cup Government cheese

1/4 cup chopped black olives

1 tablespoon all-purpose flour

1 teaspoon Italian seasonin'

1 tablespoon brandy

12 oz. SPAM, grated

Beat cream cheese until light and fluffy. Add eggs, one at a time, beatin' well after each addition. Stir in the remainin' ingredients. Fold in the SPAM.

*CRUST:*

3/4 cup seasoned bread crumbs

1/4 cup ground toasted peanuts

1/4 teaspoon nutmeg

1/4 cup margarine, melted

Combine all crust ingredients. Press into a 9-inch pie pan. Bake for 10 minutes at 350 degrees. Remove from oven, and set aside to cool for 20 minutes. Let oven cool down a bit. Pour the SPAM mixture into the cooled crust and bake for 1 hour at 300 degrees. Top with half a cup of sour cream and bake for 10 more minutes. Take it out of the oven and let it cool down to room temperature. Put in the fridge for 10 hours. Serve with crackers.

—*KITTY CHITWOOD, LOT #11*

## PUMPKIN CHEESE CAKE

*Every year the boys have a little Christmas party for all of us in the park. We drink, play white elephant or dirty Santa, and munch on fine food like this one. They really go all out. They even put red and green light bulbs in their livin' room track lightin'.*

16 oz. cream cheese

1 cup sugar

2 cans pumpkin pie fillin'

1 teaspoon cinnamon

1/2 teaspoon nutmeg

1/4 teaspoon ginger

1/8 teaspoon salt

2 beaten eggs

3 cups graham cracker crumbs

1/2 cup margarine, melted

Mix together the graham cracker crumbs and the margarine, and press them into a pie pan.

Mix the other ingredients together and pour them into the pie pan. Bake for 50 minutes at 350 degrees. Cool and top with whipped cream if desired or just serve plain.

—*DONNY OWENS, LOT #15*

## CHOCOLATE-POTATO CAKE

*I went over to the Beavers one day to pay Donna Sue's rent (she had left me a check before goin' to New Orleans with some biker gang for New Years), and there was this cake coolin' off on the table. You know me; I asked Dora what kind of cake it was. Well, without a word, she cut me off a sliver and popped it in my mouth. It was fantastic! When she told me it was made out of potatoes, I almost slipped a disk. I couldn't believe it. This cake is somethin' else!*

2 cups flour

1/2 cup cocoa

2 teaspoons bakin' powder

1/2 teaspoon salt

1/2 teaspoon cinnamon

1 cup shortenin'

2 cups sugar

4 eggs

1 cup mashed potatoes

1 teaspoon vanilla

1/3 cup milk

1 cup pecans, chopped

Stir together flour, cocoa, bakin' powder, salt, and cinnamon. Set aside. Cream shortenin' and sugar until light. Add eggs and beat until fluffy. Add potatoes and vanilla. Mix until blended. Stir in flour mixture alternately with milk. Stir in nuts. Pour into a greased 13 × 9 × 2-inch pan. Bake in a preheated oven at 350 degrees for 40 to 45 minutes. Cool in the pan. Cut into bars, and serve with ice cream or whipped cream.

—*DORA BEAVER, LOT #7*

## MOMMA BOXCAR'S CHOCOLATE SPICE CAKE

*This was the cake that won Momma her third blue ribbon.*

1/3 cup cocoa

1 teaspoon bakin' soda

3/4 cup shortenin'

2 cups sugar

1 teaspoon cloves

1 teaspoon cinnamon

1/2 cup buttermilk

3 eggs

2 cups flour

Mix together cocoa and bakin' soda. Add 1/2 cup of boilin' water and let set.

In another bowl, cream together shortenin' and sugar. Add the cocoa mixture and stir well. Mix in the remainin' ingredients. Bake in an oblong pan at 350 degrees until a toothpick can be inserted into the middle and pulled out clean. When the cake is done, remove it from the oven and punch holes in it with a fork.

Take a pan and put the followin' in it:

1 1/2 cups sugar

1/2 cup milk

1 tablespoon margarine

1 teaspoon imitation vanilla extract

Bring it to a boil. Pour over the cake. Let cool for 30 minutes and serve.

—*MOMMA BOXCAR, LOT #5*

## LOVIE'S CHINESE CAKE

*Also known as Chop Suey Cake. Don't ask me why 'cause I haven't got the slightest idea where these names came from. China maybe?*

1 cup nuts

2 cups flour

2 cups sugar

2 eggs

1 teaspoon bakin' soda

1 teaspoon salt

1 can crushed pineapple

1 stick margarine

Mix it together in a pan, and bake it as is in an oven at 350 degrees for 35 to 40 minutes. Take out of the oven and while still hot mix in the followin' ingredients:

8 oz. cream cheese

2 cups powdered sugar

1 stick margarine

1 teaspoon imitation vanilla extract

Serve as is.

—*LOVIE BIRCH, LOT #20*

# TRAILER CAKE

*This is a standard recipe that is known to all in the trailer park crowd. It is also an official trailer park recipe. It doesn't always come out right.*

2 cups flour
1 cup sugar
1 cup water
1 cup raisins
1 teaspoon imitation vanilla extract
1/3 cup CRISCO
1/2 teaspoon cloves
1 teaspoon nutmeg
1 teaspoon cinnamon
1 teaspoon bakin' soda
1/4 teaspoon salt
1/2 cup chopped nuts

You may notice there's no margarine, eggs, or milk in this recipe. It's no mistake. Put the sugar, water, and CRISCO in a bowl and boil for 2 minutes. Add bakin' soda, salt, flour, and vanilla. Bake in a loaf pan at 350 degrees until done. Serve with any frostin'.

—*DONNA SUE BOXCAR, LOT #6*

# DR PEPPER CAKE

*Guess who always asks for one of these for his birthday? That's right, my DR PEPPER drinkin' husband, Dew.*

4 tablespoons cocoa
1 1/2 teaspoons cinnamon
2 cups flour
2 cups sugar

1 cup margarine
1 cup DR PEPPER
2 eggs, well beaten
1/2 cup buttermilk
1 teaspoon bakin' soda

Mix together cocoa, cinnamon, flour, and sugar. Set aside.

Beat DR PEPPER and margarine together. Add to the dry ingredients mixture. Add eggs, buttermilk, and bakin' soda. Bake at 350 degrees for 45 minutes.

Five minutes before the cake is done, heat on a stove the followin' ingredients:

1/4 cup margarine
1/4 cup DR PEPPER
3 tablespoons cocoa

After the above is heated, add the following to it:

3 cups powdered sugar
1 teaspoon imitation vanilla extract

When the cake is done, pull it out and immediately pour the heated mixture over the cake. Let stand for 30 minutes and serve plain.

*—CONNIE KAY, LOT #13*

## THE SMALL YELLOW SCHOOL BUS CAKE

*Now this is the kind of recipe that we gals love to make. It's simple and easy.*

1 large can crushed pineapple
1 can instant cherry pie fillin'
1 box yellow cake mix
1 cup pecans, chopped
1 stick margarine

DO NOT STIR ANY OF THE INGREDIENTS TOGETHER! Spread the pineapples and their juice in an ungreased 13 × 19-inch pan.

Carefully spoon the cherry fillin' onto the pineapple layer. Sprinkle the dry yellow cake mix over the cherry fillin' layer. Place the pecans on top, and dot with margarine. Bake at 350 degrees for 1 hour. Serve plain or with vanilla ice cream.

—*LULU BELL BOXCAR, LOT #8*

## CREAM-FILLED CUPCAKES

*Ollie will put a few of these in a paper sack, and place 'em on your doorstep the night before Easter. It's her way of sharin' the good news of our Savior's resurrection. And let me tell you, if the raccoons ain't got to 'em first, they're sure nice to find on your way out the door to sunrise service.*

*Makes 30 cupcakes*
CUPCAKES:
2 1/2 cups flour
2 cups sugar
1 teaspoon bakin' powder
1/3 cup cocoa
1/4 teaspoon salt
2 eggs
1 cup oil
1 cup buttermilk
2 teaspoons bakin' soda
1 cup hot water
Stir together the flour, sugar, bakin' powder, cocoa, and salt.

Mix the eggs, oil, margarine, buttermilk, and bakin' soda, which has been dissolved in the cup of hot water, together in a bowl. Add the flour mixture and stir well.

Place muffin cups or layers in the muffin pan and fill each cup up to 2/3 full. Bake for 25 minutes at 350 degrees.

*FILLIN':*

1/2 cup sugar

1/3 cup milk

2/3 cup shortenin'

1/4 teaspoon salt

1 tablespoon water

1/2 teaspoon imitation vanilla extract

1/2 cup powdered sugar

Combine sugar, milk, shortenin', salt, water, and vanilla. Mix slowly at first, then mix on high speed for 3 to 5 minutes. Add powdered sugar and mix for another 3 to 5 minutes. Put this mixture in a frostin' tube and squirt it into each cupcake. Frost the top with a FUDGE FROSTIN'. These can be frozen.

*—OLLIE WHITE, LOT #10*

# FRUIT CAKE

*You won't find one of these cakes used after the Christmas holidays to prop open a door or hold up an open window. This is actually a fruit cake people like to eat and receive at Christmastime!*

3 1/2 cups chopped pecans

3 1/2 cups chopped walnuts

2 lbs. dates, chopped

1 lb. candied cherries, chopped

1 lb. candied pineapples, chopped

2 cans sweetened condensed milk (recipe's in the COOKIE section)

Combine all ingredients, and mix with hands. Turn into greased pans. Bake at 225 degrees for 1 1/2 hours or till cake is done. Cake is done when no milk oozes when pressed with your fingers.

*—KENNY LYNN, LOT #15*

# FUDGE CAKE

*Jeannie used to bring one of these over when her twins had done somethin' bad to you or your trailer. It was her way of sayin' "sorry." I must admit, there were a few times I blamed stuff on the Janssen boys just to get one of these. They were little demons!*

*CAKE:*

2 sticks margarine

4 tablespoons cocoa

4 eggs

2 cups sugar

1 1/2 cups flour

1/2 teaspoon salt

2 teaspoons imitation vanilla extract

Melt margarine and cocoa. Then beat eggs and sugar, add flour, salt, and cocoa mixture. Beat well. Add vanilla. Pour into greased and floured 9 × 12-inch pan. Bake at 350 for 30 minutes. Cover hot cake with marshmallows or cooled cake with this icin'.

*ICIN':*

1 stick margarine

1/4 cup cocoa

4 oz. sweetened condensed milk (Recipe's in the COOKIE section)

1 lb. powdered sugar

1 teaspoon imitation vanilla extract

Heat margarine, cocoa, and milk, then add sugar and vanilla. Mix well.

—*JEANNIE JANSSEN, LOT #19*

# PEANUT BUTTER FUDGE CAKE

*Anytime Momma wanted you to do somethin'*
*she'd always tell you if you did it she would make*
*a peanut butter fudge cake. I can't tell you how*
*many times I had to give my Me-Ma a bath!*

1 1/2 cups margarine

1/2 cup cocoa

1 cup water

1/2 cup and 6 tablespoons buttermilk

2 eggs, well beaten

2 cups sugar

2 cups flour

1 teaspoon bakin' soda

2 teaspoons imitation vanilla extract

1 1/2 cups peanut butter

1 1/2 tablespoons peanut oil

1 lb. box of powdered sugar

In a pot combine 1 cup margarine, 1/4 cup cocoa, water, 1/2 cup buttermilk, and eggs. Stir mixture constantly over low heat until it bubbles.

Mix sugar, flour, and bakin' soda. Stir the hot mixture into the dry mixture. Beat until smooth. Stir in 1 teaspoon of imitation vanilla extract. Pour into a greased and floured 13 × 9 × 2-inch pan. Bake at 350 degrees for 25 minutes or until it's puffed and firm to the touch in the center.

In another bowl mix peanut butter and peanut oil together until smooth. Spread evenly over cooled cake. In a pot, heat remainin' butter, cocoa, and buttermilk until bubbly. Place powdered sugar in a large bowl, and beat in the hot mixture. Beat until smooth. Stir in imitation vanilla extract and spread over peanut butter topping.

—*MOMMA BOXCAR, LOT #5*

# FANNY'S FUDGE CAKE

*This is Nellie's late mother's (Fanny Touchers) recipe.*

2 1/2 cups sugar
1 cup sweetened condensed milk (Recipe's in the COOKIE section)
1 1/2 cups semi-sweet chocolate chips
1/2 cup margarine
4 oz. marshmallow creme
2 teaspoons imitation vanilla extract
2 1/4 cups and 1 tablespoon flour
1 1/2 teaspoons bakin' soda
1 teaspoon salt
1/2 cup CRISCO
1/2 cup firmly packed brown sugar
3 eggs
3/4 cup milk
1/2 cup nuts

Combine sugar and milk in a pot. Cook over medium heat, stirrin' occasionally, until a little syrup dropped in cold water forms a very soft ball (230 degrees).

Place chips, margarine, marshmallow creme, and 1 teaspoon imitation vanilla extract in a large bowl, and add the sugar/milk mixture. Mix well. Chill 1 cup of this fudge and reserve the rest for frosting.

Stir together 2 1/4 cups of flour, bakin' soda, and salt.

Blend together the CRISCO and brown sugar. Make sure you cream well. Then add the eggs, one at a time, beatin' well after each. Blend in the 1 cup of chilled fudge mixture gradually, and beat well.

Combine the milk and 1 teaspoon imitation vanilla extract together. Add alternately with the dry ingredients to creamed mixture, beginnin' and endin' with dry ingredients. Blend thoroughly after each addition; if using electric mixer, use low speed.

Combine nuts and 1 tablespoon of flour. Fold into batter. Turn into two well greased and floured 9-inch round layer pans. Bake at 350 degrees for 30 to 35 minutes. Cool and frost with reserved fudge, thinned with 1 to 4 tablespoons of cream or evaporated milk, if necessary.

—*NELLIE TINKLE, LOT #4*

## GRAHAM CRACKER CAKE

*Every year the elementary school has a carnival to raise money. They sell food, play games, and even have a cake auction where you can buy a cake and eat it with the person that made it. Opal's cake always goes for a large amount because it's so darn good, but every year its buyer remains anonymous. I'm tellin' you, that poor girl is uglier than dirt! I don't know if Dottie was drinkin' or takin' some kind of medication while she was pregnant, but Opal looks like she ran through the ugly forest and hit ever tree twice. She ain't deformed or nothin', she's just ugly. Thank God she's got money!*

30 whole graham crackers
2 sticks margarine, melted
1 cup sugar
1/2 cup milk
1 egg, beaten
7 oz. can angel flake coconut
1 cup pecans, broken
1 cup graham cracker crumbs

Line bottom of dish with whole crackers.

Mix margarine, sugar, milk, and egg in a pot. Cook over medium heat, stirring constantly, until it comes to a boil. Remove from fire and add coconut, nuts, and crumbs. Spread this mixture over crackers in the dish.

Cover it with a layer of whole crackers. Serve with a BASIC ICIN' or whipped cream.

*—OPAL LAMB, LOT #14*

## DONNA SUE'S HAWAIIAN SURPRISE CAKE

*She got this one along with a case of crabs from a hitchhiker she picked up one night. We in the family refer to it as her LOVE BUG CAKE.*

2/3 cup shortenin'
2 cups sugar
2 eggs
1/2 teaspoon salt
2 cups flour
1 teaspoon bakin' soda
1 cup buttermilk
1 teaspoon imitation vanilla extract
1 can pineapple

Cream together shortenin' and 1 1/2 cups sugar until light and fluffy. Add eggs, one at a time, beatin' well after each addition. Sift together salt, flour, and soda, then add it to the shortenin' mixture alternately with the buttermilk. Add imitation vanilla extract and pour into greased 9 × 13-inch pan. Bake at 350 degrees for 20 minutes.

Five minutes before the cake is done, mix the pineapple and 1/2 cup of sugar together. When the cake is done take it out of the oven, and while it is still hot, spread the pineapple mixture over the top. Spread a HAWAIIAN ICIN' on top.

*—DONNA SUE BOXCAR, LOT #6*

# JELL-O CAKE

*This was the groom's cake at me and my husband
Dew's weddin'.*

1 box white cake mix
1 box JELL-O, any flavor
5 eggs
2/3 cup water
2/3 cup oil

Combine all the above and mix until moist on low speed, then beat for five minutes on high speed. Bake in greased tube pan for 1 hour at 350 degrees. Serve plain or with a bottle of WILD TURKEY.

—*MOMMA BALLZAK, LOT #16*

# MAYONNAISE CAKE

*I tell you, Ollie can make just about anything
taste good.*

3/4 gallon hot water (1 cup)
3/4 gallon mayonnaise (1 cup)
5 lbs. sugar (1 cup)
5 lbs. dates (1 cup)
5 lbs. nuts (1 cup)
10 lbs. flour (2 cups)

This is the cut-down recipe, which calls for a teaspoon of bakin' soda and 1/2 teaspoon of salt. Use proportionally more if you're makin' the big amount for your crowd.

Cream mayonnaise and sugar together. Pour the hot water over the dates and nuts, and add 'em to the sugar/mayonnaise mixture. Add the bakin' soda and salt to the flour and add to the above ingredients. Beat well. Bake for 35 minutes at 350 degrees. Serve with a BROWN SUGAR ICIN'.

—*OLLIE WHITE, LOT #10*

## EASY BAKE OVEN CAKE FOR ADULTS

*No light bulbs required.*

2 cups flour

1 1/2 cups sugar

2 teaspoons bakin' soda

1 medium can crushed pineapple

Mix together all the ingredients, and pour into a slightly greased 8 × 13-inch pan. Bake at 350 degrees for 30 minutes. Frost with EASY ICIN' and serve.

*—DONNY OWENS, LOT #15*

## POPCORN CHRISTMAS CAKE

*Lovie always brings this to the Christmas feedin' we hold every year at the First Baptist Church of Pangburn for the homeless. Of course we ain't got any homeless in Pangburn, so we usually invite the members of the Pangburn Lutheran Church to come over. We feed 'em first, and then we lock the doors and try to save 'em.*

4 quarts popped popcorn

1 lb. package of colored gum drops

1/2 lb. salted peanuts

1 stick margarine

1 lb. bag marshmallows

1/2 cup salad oil

Mix together the popcorn, gum drops, and peanuts. In a pot carefully melt together the margarine, marshmallows, and salad oil. While the mixture in the pot is meltin', take a tube pan and grease it. Put the popcorn mixture in the pan. When it is melted, pour the marshmallow mixture over the top of the popcorn mixture. Make sure that everything gets at least one coatin'. Press the mixture down into the pan and cover with foil to keep it moist. To serve, simply loosen the mixture with a spatula, turn the pan over and it should pop out. Decorate it as desired. (This is great for Christmastime if you use a pan that's in the shape of Santa Claus.)

*—LOVIE BIRCH, LOT #20*

## BILLY RAY CYRUS TRIBUTE
## MASHED POTATO CAKE

*This is a lot like Dora Beaver's cake, but Lulu*
*Bell insisted that I include it in my book.*

1 cup sugar
1/2 cup margarine
2 eggs, beaten
1 cup cold mashed potatoes
4 tablespoons cocoa
1 teaspoon cinnamon
1 teaspoon nutmeg
2 cups sifted flour
2 teaspoons bakin' soda
1/3 cup buttermilk
1 teaspoon imitation vanilla extract
1/2 cup walnuts, chopped
1/2 cup raisins

Cream sugar and margarine, then beat in eggs and potatoes.

Combine all the dry ingredients and add 'em to the potato mixture. Add the buttermilk and the imitation vanilla extract. Stir all together, and then add the nuts and raisins. Bake in a preheated oven at 350 degrees for 45 minutes. Serve plain.

*—LULU BELL BOXCAR, LOT #8*

## SNOWBALL CAKE

*This is great to eat durin' the winter or any other*
*time of the year.*

2 boxes gelatin
20 oz. can crushed pineapple
1 cup chopped pecans
1 cup sugar
1/4 teaspoon salt
1 day-old angel food cake
1 tub of ready-made whipped cream
1 can coconut

Dissolve the gelatin in 4 tablespoons of ice water and then add 1 cup boilin' water. Let it cool for 10 minutes. Add the pineapple, nuts, sugar, and salt. Mix and let stand in the refrigerator for about an hour, or until it's firm.

Do this next part while you're waitin' for the gelatin to firm in the fridge. Take the day-old angel food cake and cut the brown off of it (treat yourself while cookin'), and break into little pieces. Line an 11 × 9-inch pan with half the cake pieces.

Take the gelatin mixture out of the fridge and fold in the whipped cream. Pour half of the gelatin/whipped cream mixture into the lined pan. Put the rest of the cake pieces and remainin' mix over this. Sprinkle with coconut and refrigerate for 24 hours. Serve as is.

*—TAMMY CANTRELL, LOT #1*

## STRAWBERRY CAKE

*This is one of my personal favorites that Juanita*
*makes. Me and my husband, Dew, have helped*
*her and Harland out in the past when they were*
*havin' financial trouble. In return she and Har-*

*land always bring one of these cakes and the money we loaned 'em over to the trailer. Not only is the girl smart as a whip, but she can also bake like there's no tomorrow.*

1 box white cake mix
4 eggs
1 cup oil
1 package strawberry JELL-O
1 small package frozen strawberries

Soften the JELL-O in 1/2 cup of water. Combine other ingredients and blend all together with an electric mixer for at least 4 minutes. Bake in a 9 × 9 × 3-inch pan at 350 degrees for around 30 minutes or until the cake passes the toothpick test. Let the cake cool for 20 minutes on a cake rack or in the fridge. Frost the cake with STRAWBERRY ICIN'.

*—JUANITA HIX, LOT #9*

# RUBY ANN'S TOMATO SOUP CAKE

*Here it is, as promised. I love to serve this to all my Hollywood friends when they come to spend the night with me and my husband, Dew. As I hinted in the Introduction, I always end up givin' the recipe out.*

1 cup butter
1 cup sugar
1 egg
1 1/2 cups flour
1 teaspoon cinnamon
1 teaspoon nutmeg
1 teaspoon bakin' soda
1/4 teaspoon cloves
pinch salt

10 oz. can tomato soup

1 cup raisins

1 cup nuts

Cream together the butter and sugar. Add the rest of the ingredients together. Bake in a loaf pan at 350 degrees for 35 to 40 minutes or until it can pass the toothpick test. Let it cool on a rack. Once it has completely and thoroughly cooled down cover it with RUBY ANN'S FROSTIN'. When servin', don't tell anybody what it is until they've tried it. Then be ready with a camera so you can capture the look on their faces. You'll bust a gut laughin'!

—*RUBY ANN BOXCAR, LOT #18*

## SWEET TATER CAKE

*Anita brought one of these over to Me-Ma's after Pa-Pa's funeral. It was really nice of her to do, and it meant a lot to Me-Ma. Not only was it tasty, but Me-Ma was able to chew it without any problems.*

2 cups flour

2 cups sugar

1 teaspoon salt

1 teaspoon bakin' soda

1 teaspoon nutmeg

1 1/2 teaspoons cinnamon

2 teaspoons imitation vanilla extract

1/2 teaspoon cloves

1 1/4 cups oil

2 cups mashed sweet taters

4 eggs

1/2 cup pecans, chopped

Mix and bake in a pan for 1 hour and 15 minutes at 350 degrees. When it is done, slice through the middle and spread on PECAN FROSTIN'.

—*ANITA BIGGON, LOT #2*

## ME-MA'S SURPRISE CAKE

*Lord, please don't attempt this at home!*

1 store-bought cake
1 can of chocolate frosting
4 sweet pickles, chopped
1 cup tuna salad

Carefully cut off the top of the cake. Set aside. Spread the tuna salad on the topless cake. Sprinkle the pickles over the tuna salad. Put the top of the cake back on. Spread the frostin' on the entire cake. Serve with ice cream. This cake is always the talk of any gatherin' I take it to. Everybody will want to know the recipe or at least what's in it.

—*ME-MA, FORMERLY OF LOT #16*

## OLD RUGGED CROSS CAKE

*This is the official cake of the First Baptist Church*
*of Pangburn.*

2 boxes yellow cake mix

Mix up the cake accordin' to the box instructions. Take three greased loaf pans and fill them up 2/3 full. Place in the oven and cook according to the instructions on the box.

Take the remainin' cake batter and pour it into a greased muffin pan, about 2/3 full. Cook in the oven with the cake.

While these are cookin', take a 2' × 1' piece of stiff thick cardboard and cover it with foil.

When the cakes are done, take a knife and carefully cut around the loaf pans in order to loosen 'em. Turn the pans over and carefully lift the pans up to get the cakes out. Place two of the cakes in a straight line long-ways down the foil-board. Take the third cake and slice it width ways in half. Put each half at the bottom of the first cake, makin' a cross. With a knife, cut out a small wedge on each side of the top cake so that the two half cakes will fit in snuggly. Discard or eat the wedges that you've cut out. Cover all the cakes with my SANCTIFIED SOUR CREAM FROSTIN'.

Take the muffin-size cakes and place them around the bottom of the cross cake. Cover the muffin cakes with my KING DAVID CHOCO-LATE FROSTIN'. Sprinkle CHOCOLATE WAFER CREAM-FILLED COOKIE (recipe's in the COOKIE section) crumbs on top of the frosted muffin cakes.

*—SISTER BERTHA, LOT #12*

## LULU BELL'S LEMON TREE CAKE

*This is Lulu Bell's very own concoction, and I think she did dang good for a halfwit.*

1 box lemon cake mix
1 small package instant lemon puddin'
1 cup water
3/4 cup melted margarine
4 eggs

Mix everything together in a bowl. Bake it in a 9 × 13-inch pan for 35 minutes at 325 degrees. When it's done, poke some holes in the entire cake with a fork.

2 cups powdered sugar
2 tablespoons warm water
1/3 cup orange juice concentrate (undiluted)
2 tablespoons margarine, melted

Mix all these ingredients together in a bowl and pour over the cake. Make sure you cover the cake completely so that every poked hole gets some of this frostin'. Serve as is with a cold glass of milk or hot cup of coffee.

—LULU BELL BOXCAR, LOT #8

## ICIN'S, GLAZES, AND FROSTIN'S

*These are all good!*

### CARAMEL ICIN'

3 cups sugar

1 1/4 cups sweetened condensed milk, whipped (recipe's in the COOKIE section)

3 tablespoons flour

1 cup margarine

Melt 1/2 cup of sugar in a heavy skillet over low heat, stirrin' constantly, until golden brown. Set aside. In another skillet mix the rest of the sugar, milk, flour, and margarine. Cook to 225 degrees on a thermometer. Stir while cookin'. As this mixture boils, add the melted sugar. Take from the stove and frost the cake.

—OLLIE WHITE, LOT #10

### BROWN SUGAR ICIN'

2 cups brown sugar

6 tablespoons margarine

1/2 cup sweetened condensed milk, whipped (recipe's in the COOKIE section)

1 cup powdered sugar

Place brown sugar, margarine, and milk in a pot, and slowly bring it to a boil. When it's reached a full rollin' boil, remove from heat. Add powdered sugar and beat until creamy.

—OLLIE WHITE, LOT #10

## EASY ICIN'

1 can sweetened condensed milk, whipped (recipe's in the COOKIE section)
1 stick margarine
1 1/2 cups sugar
1 can angel flake coconut

Mix in pan and bring to a boil for 4 minutes. While still hot, pour over cake.

—*DONNY OWENS, LOT #15*

## EULA'S ICIN'

1 cup sugar
2 tablespoons flour
1 teaspoon imitation vanilla extract
1 teaspoon nutmeg
1/2 teaspoon cinnamon
1 cup water
2 tablespoons margarine

Mix all together and bring to a boil. Boil for 3 minutes. Cool and frost.

—*MABLE SKAGGS, LOT #17*

## 7 MINUTE ICIN'

2 egg whites
1 1/2 cups sugar
5 tablespoons cold water
1/4 teaspoon cream of tartar
1 teaspoon imitation vanilla extract

Put egg whites, sugar, water, and cream of tartar in the upper part of a double-boiler. Beat with an egg beater until thoroughly mixed. Place over rapidly boilin' water, beatin' constantly with the egg beater. Cook for 7 minutes. Remove it from the fire, add imitation vanilla extract, and beat until it is thick enough to spread.

—*DORA BEAVER, LOT #7*

## BASIC ICIN'

1 stick margarine
6 tablespoons milk
2 cups powdered sugar
1 teaspoon imitation vanilla extract
Beat with mixer until fluffy.

—*OPAL LAMB, LOT #14*

## HAWAIIAN ICIN'

1 1/2 cups sugar
1/2 cup water
1 tablespoon white corn syrup
2 egg whites
Combine sugar, water, and corn syrup in a pot, and cook to soft ball stage or 238 degrees on a candy thermometer. Beat egg whites until they stand in soft peaks and thread syrup in to whites, beatin' constantly. Continue to beat for about 3 minutes. Spread over your cake or cupcakes and sprinkle with coconut.

—*DONNA SUE BOXCAR, LOT #6*

## BUTTERMILK ICIN'

3 cups sugar
2 sticks margarine
1 cup buttermilk
2 tablespoons light corn syrup

1 teaspoon bakin' soda
1 cup pecans, finely chopped
In a 4-quart pot, over medium heat, heat the sugar, margarine, butter-milk, corn syrup, and bakin' soda to a boil. Stir constantly. Cook until it reaches 238 degrees on a candy thermometer. Pour the mixture into a large bowl and beat at high speed for 7 minutes. Fold in the pecans.

*—TAMMY CANTRELL, LOT #1*

## STRAWBERRY ICIN'

1/2 stick margarine
1 box confectioners sugar
1 small package frozen strawberries
Cream margarine and sugar. Add as much of the drained frozen straw-berries as the mixture will take.

*—JUANITA HIX, LOT #9*

## LEMON ICIN'

1 cup sugar
1/2 cup flour
1 cup boilin' water
1 tablespoon lemon juice
3 tablespoons margarine
Mix sugar and flour together. Make a paste with 1/4 cup of water and the sugar/flour mixture. Add paste to the boilin' water and cook until thick. Let it cool and then add the lemon juice and margarine.

*—JEANNIE JANSSEN, LOT #19*

## SUGAR GLAZE

1 cup powdered sugar
1 teaspoon margarine
Milk
Mix together and add enough milk to get it to your desired thickness.
—*LOIS BUNCH, LOT #3*

## ORANGE GLAZE

Same as the SUGAR GLAZE, but use orange juice instead of milk to get the desired thickness.
—*LOIS BUNCH, LOT #3*

## KING DAVID CHOCOLATE FROSTIN'

1 cup margarine
1 can sweetened condensed milk, whipped (recipe's in the COOKIE section)
2 cups sugar
1/2 cup semi-sweet chocolate chips
1 teaspoon imitation vanilla extract
Combine margarine, milk, and sugar in a medium-size pot. Bring to a boil and let cook for 3 minutes over medium heat. Stir constantly. Stir in chocolate chips and imitation vanilla extract. Beat with a spoon until creamy and until it has reached a spreadin' consistency.
—*SISTER BERTHA, LOT #12*

## PECAN FROSTIN'

1/2 stick margarine
3 oz. cream cheese

1/2 box powdered sugar
1/2 cup pecans, chopped
2 teaspoons imitation vanilla extract
Mix it all together until creamy. Let stand for 5 minutes or until it thickens. Spread on cake.

—*ANITA BIGGON, LOT #2*

## RUBY ANN'S FROSTIN'

8 oz. cream cheese
1 tablespoon margarine
1 tablespoon milk
Powdered sugar
Mix together and add just enough powdered sugar to make smooth.

—*RUBY ANN BOXCAR, LOT #18*

## BUTTER FROSTIN'

1/3 cup margarine
4 1/2 cups powdered sugar
1/4 cup milk
1 1/2 teaspoons imitation vanilla extract
Beat margarine till fluffy. Gradually add 2 cups of the powdered sugar, beatin' well. Slowly beat in the 1/4 cup milk and imitation vanilla extract. Slowly beat in remainin' sugar. Beat in additional milk if needed, to get to a spreadin' consistency.

—*KITTY CHITWOOD, LOT #11*

## PACKED FUDGE FROSTIN'

4 3/4 cups powdered sugar
1/2 cup cocoa
1 stick margarine, softened

1/3 cup boilin' water

1 teaspoon imitation vanilla extract

Mix powdered sugar and cocoa. Add margarine, boilin' water, and imitation vanilla extract. Beat with an electric mixer on low speed till combined. Beat for 1 minute on medium speed. Cool for 20 to 30 minutes. You can also pack the fudge up and freeze it for later use (no more than a month). Set it out and let it thaw to room temperature before usin'.

—*KENNY LYNN, LOT #15*

## SANCTIFIED SOUR CREAM FROSTIN'

1 cube margarine, softened

3 cups powdered sugar

1/2 cup sour cream

2 teaspoons imitation vanilla extract

Mix together ingredients. Beat on high until smooth and fluffy, about 5 minutes.

—*SISTER BERTHA, LOT #12*

# Chapter 8

**Jell-O Divinity** sure helps Sister Bertha of lot #12
put a smile on little Dick Hickey, Pastor Hickey's son.

# *Candy*

There are three things I remember about my late Granny Boxcar (my daddy's momma) who passed away when I was six years old: She was only 4 feet tall, she didn't have a forehead, and she always had candy in the house. She died when her washin' machine went haywire and began whirlin' violently across the floor durin' a spin cycle, crushin' her tiny frame up against the utility room wall. Daddy said that when they found her lifeless body she had a bottle of fabric softener in one hand and a piece of half-eaten chocolate fudge in the other. That old woman loved candy, and I guess I've inherited that sweet tooth of hers, especially when it comes to fudge. Granny Boxcar use to call her chocolate fudge BOXCAR'S FLAWLESS FANTASY FUDGE 'cause it was truly flawless. But seein' how Granny Boxcar and my momma never got along, she refused to pass down any of the Boxcar family recipes to my side of the family. Momma always made her own momma's recipe, which tasted like a dried-out brick of chocolate fudge dust (Me-Ma was never good at candy makin' thus it's not Momma's specialty either). Because of their argument, the BOXCAR'S FLAWLESS FANTASY FUDGE and it's recipe died pinned up against that utility wall with Granny. So I played around in my trailer kitchen until, back in 1972, I came up with a fudge that tastes even better than Granny Boxcar's long-gone fudge. RUBY ANN BOXCAR'S FANTASTICALLY FLAWLESS FANTASY FUDGE is based on the taste that I can still remember to this day.

Even though my granny never lived in a trailer home, she had the mind of a trailer dweller. I say this because you'll always find some form of candy when you visit one of us in the High Chaparral Trailer Park. Usually we keep a little bit set out in a fancy colored glass candy dish like you win at the fair. It's like what Granny Boxcar once told me when I asked her about all the candy she had around the house. She looked up at me and said, "Darlin', nothin' says your welcomed here like a little bit of candy and an open jug of your Grandpa's moonshine."

## BON-BONS

*You'll have a hard time keepin' these in a candy dish for long.*

1 quart pecan meats, chopped
2 sticks margarine
1 can sweetened condensed milk (recipe is in the COOKIE section)
2 boxes powdered sugar
1 block canning wax
1 package chocolate chips

Mix well the pecans, margarine, milk, and powdered sugar. Roll into little balls and place on a wax paper–covered cookie sheet. Place in the fridge and let cool overnight.

On the next day, melt the canning wax and chocolate chips in a double broiler. Dip the balls in the melted mixture and replace on the wax papered cookie sheet. Let 'em stand till they've set.

—*DONNY OWENS, LOT #15*

## EULA'S CANDY BARS

*This tastes like a candy bar we've known for years.*

1/2 cup white sugar
1/2 cup brown sugar
1 cup white syrup
1 cup peanut butter
6 cups corn flakes
1 cup salted peanuts

6 oz. semi-sweet chocolate chips

6 oz. milk chocolate chips

In a pot mix white sugar, brown sugar, and syrup over low heat. Bring it to a boil and cook for 1 minute. Take off the heat and add peanut butter. Stir well. In a large mixin' bowl stir together corn flakes and peanuts. Add the sugar/syrup mixture and mix. Grease up a 9 × 13-inch pan and firmly press the mixture into the pan.

Melt both types of chips and pour over the pressed mixture that's in the pan. Put it in the fridge and let cool for about an hour. Cut into squares and serve.

—*MABLE SCAGGS, LOT #17*

## BUCK-EYE CANDY

*These will remind you of a certain candy that is usually in a cup form.*

1/2 cup margarine, softened

1/8 teaspoon salt

1 1/2 cups peanut butter

1 teaspoon imitation vanilla extract

16 oz. powdered sugar

3 tablespoons shortenin'

12 oz. semi-sweet chocolate chips

1/2 stick paraffin wax

Combine the salt and margarine. Add the peanut butter and vanilla extract. Mix well until it makes a stiff dough. If needed, add 1 tablespoon of water. Shape into small flat circular pieces and place on wax paper. Put in the fridge and let chill for 10 to 15 minutes.

Melt the shortenin', chips, and paraffin wax. Carefully dip the flat pieces in the melted mixture and place on wax paper to set.

—*KENNY LYNN, LOT #15*

## RUBY ANN'S PEANUT BUTTER BALLS

*My husband, Dew, just loves these little balls of*
*joy! I like to put 'em in the freezer before I eat 'em.*
*Frozen or not, these balls are great.*

2 sticks margarine
1 cup peanut butter
1 lb. powdered sugar
1 cup graham cracker crumbs
1 large milk chocolate candy bar
6 oz. chocolate chips
1 square paraffin wax

Cream together the margarine and peanut butter. Add the powdered sugar and graham cracker crumbs. Blend together with your clean (optional) hands and roll into small balls.

Melt the candy bar, chocolate chips, and paraffin wax in a double boiler. Carefully dip each ball into the melted mixture, and place 'em on a piece of wax paper. Let 'em cool and enjoy.

—*RUBY ANN BOXCAR, LOT #18*

## CANDIED CRACKERS

*These are just as good as the ones that are made in*
*that rotted out tree by them small people with*
*pointy ears, if you catch my drift.*

1/2 cup margarine
1/4 cup brown sugar
12 single squares graham crackers
1 cup milk chocolate chips
1/2 cup nuts, chopped

Put the margarine and brown sugar in a pot and bring to a boil over a medium heat. Cook for 2 minutes. Cool for 5 minutes.

Place the graham cracker squares in a shallow pan. Pour the mixture over the crackers and bake at 375 degrees for 5 minutes. Remove from the oven and sprinkle on the chips and nuts. Allow the bars to cool and cut 'em in half.

*—LOVIE WHITE, LOT #20*

# JELL-O DIVINITY

*This candy is as close to heaven as a non-Baptist can get!*

3 cups sugar
3/4 cup water
3/4 cup white syrup
3 egg whites
1 package JELL-O, any flavor
1 cup nuts

Bring the sugar, water, and syrup to a hard boil (252 degrees on the candy thermometer). Beat the egg whites till very stiff then add the dry JELL-O. Add the syrup mixture and beat until stiff. Add the nuts. Spread on a greased dish and let it cool.

*—SISTER BERTHA, LOT #12*

# RUBY ANN BOXCAR'S FANTASTICALLY FLAWLESS FANTASY FUDGE

*Please don't send me letters tellin' me how good this fudge is, 'cause I already know. Heck, just look at me!*

8 oz. semi-sweet chocolate chips
2/3 cup sweetened condensed milk (recipe is in the COOKIE section)
1 teaspoon imitation vanilla extract
1/4 teaspoon salt
1/2 cup nuts, chopped

Heat milk and chips in a pot on low heat until the chips are melted. Stir constantly. Remove from the heat and stir in the imitation vanilla extract and salt. Stir in the nuts and spread in a greased pan. Chill for 30 minutes or until firm.

—*RUBY ANN BOXCAR, LOT #18*

## NO COOK CHEESE NUT FUDGE

*This stuff is the deal on those nights you get a hankerin' for some fudge, and you want it now!*

3 oz. cream cheese, softened

2 1/2 cups confectioners' sugar

1/4 teaspoon imitation almond extract

1/2 cup almonds, pecans, or walnuts, chopped

Grease a 9 × 5-inch loaf pan with margarine. In a small bowl, beat the cream cheese, sugar, and imitation almond extract until smooth. Stir in the nuts and spread in the pan. Refrigerate for 30 minutes and cut into squares.

—*NELLIE TINKLE, LOT #4*

## DORA BEAVER'S BLUE RIBBON PEANUT BUTTER FUDGE

*If your teeth ain't already rottin' out of your head, this stuff will do it!*

1 can sweetened condensed milk (recipe is in the COOKIE section)

1 1/2 sticks margarine

3 cups sugar

7 oz. marshmallow creme

18 oz. creamy peanut butter

Put the milk, margarine and sugar in a pot and bring to a rolling boil on medium heat. Stir constantly until the mixture reaches 234 degrees on a candy thermometer. Take it off the heat and stir in the marshmallow creme and peanut butter. Pour it into a greased pan and let it stand until it cools.

—*DORA BEAVER, LOT #7*

# LULU BELL'S PERFECT PINEAPPLE FUDGE

*She brought this back from one of those Carnival
Cruises she took in an unsuccessful attempt to find
her idol, Kathy Lee Gifford.*

3 cups sugar
1 tablespoon light corn syrup
8 oz. pineapple, crushed and drained
1/2 cup whippin' cream
1 tablespoon margarine
1/2 teaspoon imitation vanilla extract
1 cup black walnuts, coarsely chopped

Combine sugar, syrup, pineapple, and whippin' cream in a pot that has been well buttered with margarine. Cook over a medium flame, stirrin' occasionally, until it reaches 236 degrees. Remove from heat and add the tablespoon of margarine. DO NOT STIR! Let the candy set and cool until lukewarm. Add the imitation vanilla. Beat until candy begins to thicken. Stir in the walnuts and pour into a greased pan. Cool and cut into squares.

—*LULU BELL BOXCAR, LOT #8*

# TRAILER FUDGE

*This fudge is almost as good as mine. Note the
word* almost!

1 can sweetened condensed milk (recipe is in the COOKIE section)
1 teaspoon imitation vanilla extract
12 oz. semi-sweet chocolate chips
6 oz. butterscotch chips
2 cups pecans, finely chopped

Put the milk, imitation vanilla, and both kinds of chips in a pot over hot water till all the chips are melted. Add the pecans and pour into a greased pan. Store in the icebox until slightly firm. Cut into squares and put back in the icebox until it's hard.

—*WANDA RAY, LOT #13*

## EULA'S WHITE RIVER FUDGE

*This fudge is so good it'll kill you.*

1 can sweetened condensed milk (recipe is in the COOKIE section)
1/4 cup light corn syrup
3 cups granulated sugar
1/2 teaspoon salt
1 teaspoon imitation vanilla extract
2 tablespoons margarine
1/4 cup pecans, chopped

Put the milk, corn syrup, sugar, and salt in a deep pot. Cook, stirrin' constantly, until the mixture reaches 236 degrees on a candy thermometer. Add the imitation vanilla and margarine. Set the pot in cold water until the mixture starts thickenin', and then stir in the nuts. Pour into a greased pan, spreadin' evenly. Cut into squares and put in the fridge till it hardens.

*—MABLE SCAGGS, LOT #17*

## PEANUT BRITTLE

*Lord, I could, and have eaten a whole batch of
this stuff all by myself!*

1 cup white syrup
2 cups raw peanuts, shelled
2 teaspoons bakin' soda
2 cups sugar
1 cup water
1 teaspoon margarine
1/2 teaspoon imitation vanilla extract

Cook sugar, water, syrup and peanuts until mixture breaks when dropped in cool water. Stir in the bakin' soda and vanilla. Beat rapidly until the bakin' soda is mixed in well. Take a cookie sheet and butter it up with margarine. Sprinkle additional sugar over the cookie sheet. Pour the peanut brittle mixture over the cookie sheet. Let cool and enjoy.

*—JUANITA HIX, LOT #9*

## PEANUT BUTTER CANDY

*I pass these out to the kids that come knockin' at my door on Halloween.*

2 cups sugar
1/2 cup milk
6 tablespoons peanut butter
24 graham crackers, finely crumbled

Mix the sugar and milk in a pot and bring to a rolling boil. Remove from the heat and add peanut butter and graham crackers. Beat the mixture until it's creamy. Pour out into small bar-shaped forms on a greased cookie sheet. Let the bars cool till they're hardened. If you like you can dip these bars into some melted chocolate and paraffin wax and place 'em on wax paper to cool.

—*TAMMY CANTRELL, LOT #1*

## PECAN LOG

*These will bring back memories of those old convenient store/restaurants that used to be on every highway.*

7 oz. marshmallow creme
1 teaspoon imitation vanilla extract
1/4 teaspoon imitation almond extract
1 lb. powdered sugar
1 lb. caramels
1 lb. pecans, chopped

Add extracts to marshmallow creme and gradually sift the powdered sugar in. Knead the sugar and marshmallow creme mixture. Shape into 4 × 6 1-inch cylinders. Wrap and freeze.

Melt the caramels in a double boiler. Dip the frozen cylinders in the hot melted caramel. Immediately roll in chopped nuts. Cool and then wrap in wax paper and place in the fridge.

—*LOIS BUNCH, LOT #3*

# Chapter 9

Ollie White of lot #10 sure gives those little girls a run for their money each year with her own **Thin Mint Cookies**.

# *Cookies*

In the world of the trailer park, if one of your neighbors gets sick or dies, you always take cookies over to the family members. Why cookies? Well it's simple. It's a hell of lot cheaper to make a batch of cookies then it is to make a cake or a pie. Plus if you decide while cookin' that you want to take a bit or two, who's going to miss a few cookies? If there's a big slice of pie or cake missin' everybody'll notice. Even for us, that'd be rude! So when you got to cook somethin' that you'll be givin' away to somebody else, it's always cookies. The only exception to this rule is when it's a sit down potluck dinner and you've got to bring a dish. Cookies are not appropriate in this case. After all, if you bring cookies to a potluck dinner, then you can't complain about the other folks that brought cookies as a dish.

There are only a few times when you will buy cookies: if your recipe calls for vanilla wafers and you don't feel like makin' 'em yourself, if the Piggly Wiggly's havin' a sale on crushed packages of OREO cookies (all of us have an OREO clone recipe), and when them Girl Scouts come knockin' at your door (this is one of my favorite times of the year). Other than those three times, you make your own.

## SWEETENED CONDENSED MILK

*This recipe will save you a ton of money.*

1 cup plus 2 tablespoons powdered milk
3/4 cup sugar
1/2 cup water

Combine all the above ingredients in a pan and heat to a boil. Cook for 15 to 20 minutes or until it's thick. This will make one can's worth.

—*NELLIE TINKLE, LOT #4*

# BANANA COOKIES

*I like to slap a little bit of my own RUBY ANN*
*FROSTIN' on the tops of these cookies after lettin'*
*'em cool for just a few minutes.*

1 1/2 cups sifted flour
1 cup sugar
1/2 teaspoon bakin' soda
1 teaspoon salt
1/4 teaspoon nutmeg
1 teaspoon cinnamon
3/4 cup oil
1 egg, well beaten
1 cup mashed bananas
1 3/4 cups oatmeal
1/2 package chocolate chips

Sift together all dry ingredients. Add oil, egg, bananas, oatmeal, and chocolate chips. Mix well. Drop by teaspoon on ungreased cookie sheet, and bake for 10 to 12 minutes at 350 degrees.

—*MOMMA BALLZAK, LOT #16*

# RUBY ANN'S TOP DOG BROWNIES

*These will make you sit up and beg for more.*

3 eggs
1 stick margarine, softened
1 box chocolate cake or fudge cake mix
Cocoa

1 lb. powdered sugar

8 oz. cream cheese

Mix together 1 egg and the margarine. Add the cake mix. Take a greased 13 × 9-inch bakin' pan and flour it with cocoa instead of flour. This will prevent the sides from comin' out white. Spread the mixture in the pan.

Beat the powdered sugar, cream cheese, and the two eggs together until creamy. Spread on top of the cake mixture that's already in the pan. Put in the oven and bake at 350 degrees for 50 minutes. When done, cut into smalls squares and serve. It's rich and it won't take a lot to satisfy even those with large appetites.

—*RUBY ANN BOXCAR, LOT #18*

## CARROT COOKIES

*Lovie serves these at her annual Democratic Christmas Party. I've seen people change political affiliations just to get a taste of these.*

3/4 cup sugar

3/4 cup shortenin'

1 egg

1 1/4 cup grated raw carrots

2 cups sifted flour

2 teaspoons bakin' powder

1/2 teaspoon salt

1 teaspoon imitation vanilla extract

1/2 teaspoon lemon extract

Cream together the sugar and shortenin' until fluffy. Add the egg and beat well. Stir in the carrots. Sift together the dry ingredients and combine with the cream mixture. Add the imitation vanilla and lemon extract. Drop by the teaspoonful on a greased cookie sheet. Bake for 15 minutes at 375 degrees.

—*LOVIE WHITE, LOT #20*

## THE KING'S CHEESE COOKIES

*This is not one of the king's personal recipes, and the officials at Graceland have not approved it. We just named 'em that because Anita always brings these to the Sweat Scarves of Elvis fan club meetin's.*

1/4 lb. margarine
8 oz. cream cheese
1 tablespoon sugar
1 egg
1 cup flour
1/2 cup sugar
1 cup chopped nuts
Cinnamon to taste

Cream margarine and cream cheese. Mix all ingredients well. Roll out on a floured cloth and sprinkle with cup sugar, chopped nuts, and cinnamon. Roll as jelly roll and chill overnight. Slice and bake at 350 degrees for 8 to 10 minutes.

—*ANITA BIGGON, LOT #2*

## CHOCOLATE COOKIE WAFERS

*Momma would reward us kids with a batch of these if we did good on our report cards. I don't recall Donna Sue ever eatin' one of these.*

1 box fudge cake mix
2 tablespoons water
2 tablespoons oil
2 eggs
1/2 cup cocoa
1/4 cup water

Mix all the above ingredients together until smooth. Let stand for around 25 to 30 minutes. Roll into little balls and put 'em on a greased cookie sheet. Take a glass and grease the bottom of it. Dip the greased bottom of the glass into some instant chocolate drink powder (the kind you use to make chocolate milk). Flatten each cookie with the glass bottom (make sure you redip the glass bottom after flattenin' each ball). Bake for 8 to 10 minutes at 400 degrees. When you take the cookies out of the oven, flatten the cookies again with a clean glass bottom or spatula. Let 'em cool.

—*MOMMA BOXCAR, LOT #5*

## WANDA'S CHOCOLATE DROP COOKIES

1/2 cup shortenin', melted
1 cup brown sugar, packed
1 egg
2 squares chocolate, melted
1 3/4 cups flour
1/4 teaspoon bakin' soda
1 teaspoon bakin' powder
1/2 cup milk
1/2 teaspoon imitation vanilla extract

Cream shortenin' and sugar. Add the egg and chocolate. Combine the flour, bakin' soda, and bakin' powder, siftin' 'em together. Add milk and vanilla to the sugar/shortenin' mixture and mix in the flour mixture. Beat well. Drop spoonfuls on a greased cookie sheet. Bake at 350 degrees for 10 to 12 minutes.

—*WANDA KAY, LOT #13*

## CHOCOLATE WAFER CREAM-FILLED COOKIES

*I incorporated Momma's wafer recipe to create a*
*cookie that tastes just like the ones you can buy at*
*the store.*

Use the CHOCOLATE COOKIE WAFER recipe for the cookie part.
*CREAM FILLIN':*
3 oz. unflavored gelatin
1/4 cup cold water
1 cup shortenin'
5 cups confectioners sugar
1 teaspoon imitation vanilla extract
Put the gelatin in the water and slowly heat on simmer until it clears.
Cream together the shortenin' and confectioners sugar. Add the imitation
vanilla extract and the cooled down gelatin. Beat well. Put the fillin' on one
of the chocolate wafers. Place another wafer on top of this and carefully
press 'em together.

*—RUBY ANN BOXCAR, LOT #18*

## CORNFLAKE COOKIES

*These are also great when you use the sugar-*
*coated cornflakes.*

1 cup shortenin'
1 cup white sugar
1 cup brown sugar
2 eggs
1 tablespoon milk
1 teaspoon imitation vanilla extract
Cream well, then add:
2 cups flour
1 teaspoon bakin' soda

1/2 teaspoon bakin' powder
1/2 teaspoon salt
Mix well, and add:
2 cups cornflakes
2 cups oats
1 cup pecans, chopped
1 cup coconut
Mix well. Spoon onto ungreased cookie sheet. Bake at 350 degrees for 8 to 10 minutes or until lightly golden brown.

—*JEANNIE JANSSEN, LOT #19*

## FUDGE COOKIES

*These are always the top sellers at the Pangburn Elementary School carnival.*

1/2 cup shortenin', melted
1 cup cocoa
2 cups sugar
4 eggs
1/4 cup margarine, melted
2 teaspoons imitation vanilla extract
2 cups flour
2 teaspoons bakin' powder
1/4 teaspoon salt
3/4 cup nuts

Combine shortenin' and cocoa together. Add sugar, eggs, margarine, and imitation vanilla extract. Beat well. Sift dry ingredients and mix with the first mixture. Add the nuts and mix well. Chill several hours. Make into balls and then roll 'em in powdered sugar. Place on a greased cookie sheet. Bake 10 to 20 minutes at 350 degrees. Let 'em cool for 5 minutes for easy removal from the cookie sheet.

—*LOIS BUNCH, LOT #3*

## HELLO DARLIN' COOKIE SQUARES

*My sister came up with these when she was datin'
a Conway Twitty impersonator who did a show
in one of those smaller bars in Reno. That rela-
tionship lasted about a year and a half. The last
we heard, he had put on 60 pounds and was im-
personatin' Wayne Newton in Branson, Missouri.*

1 stick margarine
1 cup graham cracker crumbs
1 cup shredded coconut
6 oz. butterscotch chips
6 oz. chocolate chips
1/2 cup pecans
1 can sweetened condensed milk

Take a 13 × 9 × 2-inch bakin' pan and put the slightly melted margarine
in it. One at a time, place all the other ingredients in it as listed in order
above. Make sure you sprinkle each ingredient out as you put it in the pan.
DO NOT MIX THE INGREDIENTS TOGETHER. Bake for 30 min-
utes at 350 degrees. When finished baking, cut into squares.

*—DONNA SUE BOXCAR, LOT #6*

## HONEY-ROASTED PEANUT CLUSTERS

*If you should win at bingo, and have some extra
money, substitute the honey roasted cashews for
honey roasted peanuts!*

1/2 cup peanut butter
1 cup semi-sweet chocolate chips
1 cup honey-roasted peanuts

Combine peanut butter and chocolate chips in the top of a double
boiler, and place 'em over tap hot (NOT BOILING) water until melted.
Stir until they blend together. Add the honey-roasted peanuts and stir

until they're well coated. Drop by the spoonful onto wax paper. Chill until set.

*—JUANITA HIX, LOT #9*

## DOTTIE LAMB'S LEMON COOKIES

*These are the same ones she sells in the LAMB DEPARTMENT STORE!*

3/4 cup margarine
3/4 cup sugar
1 egg, slightly beaten
1 teaspoon lemon flavorin'
1/2 teaspoon bakin' soda
1/2 teaspoon salt
1/2 teaspoon cream of tartar
2 cups all-purpose flour

Cream margarine and sugar together. Add the egg and lemon flavorin'. Sift the dry ingredients together and add to the creamed mixture. Roll into balls and dip 'em in sugar. Place the balls on a cookie sheet. Press each cookie with a fork. Bake at 350 degrees for 10 minutes.

*—DOTTIE LAMB, LOT #14*

## NO BAKIN' COOKIES

*These are so easy to make, I'd let my Me-Ma make these without supervision.*

2 cups sugar
1 stick margarine
1/2 cup cocoa
1/2 cup milk
1/2 cup peanut butter
4 cups 3-minute oats

Bring sugar, margarine, cocoa, and milk to a rollin' boil, and cook for 1 minute. Remove from fire and add peanut butter and oats. Blend thoroughly. Drop from teaspoon onto wax paper. Let 'em cool.

*—LULU BELL BOXCAR, LOT #8*

## OLLIE'S THIN MINT COOKIES

*Just like the kind them little girls in the green uniforms sell.*

*MAKES ABOUT 100 COOKIES (25 TO 30)*

30 oz. chocolate mint chips (7 oz.)

1/2 cup shortenin' (2 tablespoons)

Put the above ingredients into a double boiler and melt over hot water. Stir and heat until it's smooth. Carefully dip a chocolate cookie wafer (included in this section) in the mixture. Place it on wax paper. Let 'em cool until they set.

*—OLLIE WHITE, LOT #10*

## TRAILER PARK BASIC COOKIE RECIPE

*This recipe can be used for any kind of cookie.*

3 cups flour

3 teaspoons bakin' powder

3/4 teaspoon salt

3/4 teaspoon margarine, melted

2 eggs

1 teaspoon imitation vanilla extract

1 1/3 cup sweetened condensed milk

YOUR FAVORITE FLAVORIN'

Take a large mixing bowl and put sifted blended dry ingredients in it. Stir in the rest of the ingredients, with the exception of YOUR FAVORITE FLAVORIN'. Mix well. Fold in YOUR FAVORITE FLAVORIN' and drop level tablespoons of dough about two inches apart on a well-greased cookie sheet. Bake at 350 degrees for 8 to 10 minutes. Remove at once from the cookie sheet when done.

YOUR FAVORITE FLAVORIN' could be one of the followin':

6 oz. semi-sweet chocolate chips

1 1/2 cups seedless raisins

1 1/2 cups sugar-coated cornflakes

1 1/2 cups minature marshmallows

1 1/2 cups peanut butter cups

1 1/2 cups shredded coconut

1 1/2 cups pineapple, crushed or cubed

1 1/2 cups milk chocolate, chopped

1 1/2 cups dried dates

1 1/2 cups fudge

1 1/2 cups sugar-coated chocolate pieces

1 1/2 cups butterscotch candy, crushed

1 1/2 cups cherries or any of your favorite candies or fruits.

—*NELLIE TINKLE, LOT #4*

## TWO-TIMIN' BEER COOKIES

*The smell of these babies will have him comin'*
*straight home at night!*

1/2 cup brown sugar

1/2 cup margarine

2 cups flour

1/2 cup bakin' soda

1 teaspoon cinnamon

1 1/4 cups beer that's been left open overnight at room temperature

1/2 cup nuts (pecans or walnuts)

Cream together the margarine and brown sugar. Add the flour, bakin' soda, and cinnamon. Mix well. Slowly add the beer. Blend well. Drop teaspoonfuls of dough on a greased cookie sheet. Top with nuts. Bake for 12 minutes or until golden brown at 350 degrees.

—*KITTY CHITWOOD, LOT #11*

## VANILLA WAFER COOKIES

*Just like the ones that come in the box.*

1/2 cup powdered sugar
1/3 cup sugar
1/3 cup shortenin'
1 egg
1 teaspoon imitation vanilla extract
1/8 teaspoon salt
1 1/2 cups flour
1 1/2 teaspoons bakin' powder
1 tablespoon water

In a large bowl combine the powdered sugar, sugar, shortenin', egg, imitation vanilla extract, and salt. Mix in the flour and bakin' powder. Mix well. Add about a tablespoon of water and mix. Roll the dough into little balls and place 'em on a greased cookie sheet. Flatten 'em with your hand. Bake at 325 degrees for 15 minutes or until they reach the desired golden brown color like the ones that come in the box.

—*TAMMY CANTRELL, LOT #1*

## VIRGIN MARY MOLASSES COOKIES

*Sister Bertha always makes it a point to let everybody know that she ain't turned Catholic or nothin' when she serves these cookies. She reminds us all that Mary was the mother of Jesus, and that the Bible says Mary was a virgin at the time of his birth. So accordin' to Sister Bertha, these cookies are about as Catholic as Christianity.*

1/2 cup brown sugar
1 1/2 cups dark molasses
1 cup shortenin', melted
1 cup hot water
5 cups flour
1 teaspoon ginger
3 teaspoons bakin' soda

Mix first four ingredients together. Sift flour, ginger, and bakin' soda together, then add to first mixture. Refrigerate for about 4 hours or overnight. Roll out thin and with a butter knife, cut into the shape of the Virgin Mary. Take a spatula and carefully lift each virgin up and place her on a greased cookie sheet. Put in the oven and bake at 375 degrees for 10 to 12 minutes.

—*SISTER BERTHA, LOT #12*

# Chapter 10

Mickey Ray Kay and his momma, Wanda Kay, just love Mickey's
wife Connie's **DR PEPPER SALAD** down at lot #13.

# *Desserts*

Durin' my many travels outside of Pangburn, Arkansas, I've learned that non-trailer livin' people tend to finish off a meal with a dessert. This was not only strange to me, but also a bit odd. To this day I still don't understand why people would want to make the dessert the last course of their meal. Maybe we trailer park folks are just backwards, but we eat dessert before, durin', after, or even without a havin' a meal. We don't hold to some set time of when we got to eat our desserts. I've actually seen some non-trailer park livin' people pass on desserts all together! They were too full from everything else they had eaten to take part in the dessert! Talk about your nutcases! This would never, and I do mean never, happen in a trailer park. Even when somebody in a trailer park tells you they're not hungry, they'll still eat some dessert. When I got back home and told my neighbors what I had seen, they all thought I was lyin'. They couldn't imagine such a thing. Now from time to time I've been guilty of smokin' a cigarette before eatin' my dessert, but to pass on it all together just ain't right. I guess this is a part of our two cultures that we'll never see eye to eye on it. Passin' on dessert. I'm tellin' you there is somethin' wrong with you people!

## APPLE CRISP

*There are five things you can count on at the Box-car family Christmas gatherin': gettin' a present that will be returned on the next day, everybody tellin' you how much they spent on your gift,*

*Donna Sue smellin' of cheap booze, Me-Ma's bla-*
*tant flatulence, and Momma's fresh hot apple crisp.*

4 cups apples, peeled and sliced
1 cup sugar
3/4 cup flour
1 teaspoon cinnamon
1/2 teaspoon salt
1/2 cup margarine
1 cup oatmeal or graham cracker crumbs

Place the apples in a margarine-coated pan. Sift together sugar, flour, and cinnamon and cut in the 1/2 cup of margarine. Stir in the oatmeal or crumbs. The mixture should be crumbly. Sprinkle the mixture over the apples and bake uncovered at 350 degrees for 1 hour. Top with vanilla ice cream when servin'.

—*MOMMA BOXCAR, LOT #5*

## GRANNY VERLINA'S APPLE FRITTERS

*This is a recipe from my husband's late Granny*
*Verlina Pruitt. We thought she took it to the grave*
*with her until Momma Ballzak got plastered one*
*night and had a flashback that she was helping*
*Granny Verlina cook these lovely delights. I jotted*
*down the recipe while she rambled on. I'd give it*
*to Momma Ballzak, but me and my husband,*
*Dew, don't let her cook with hot grease since the*
*time she was frying a summer sausage and acci-*
*dentally caught her cat on fire. Don't worry, Puss-*
*Puss is fine!*

1 cup flour
2 tablespoons sugar
dash salt
1 teaspoon bakin' powder

2 eggs, slightly beaten

2/3 cup milk

1 teaspoon oil

4 to 6 tart cookin' apples, peeled

Powdered sugar

Sift together flour, 2 tablespoons of sugar, salt, and bakin' powder. Combine eggs, milk, and the oil. Add to the sugar mixture, and beat until it's smooth. Take the apples and core 'em. Slice 'em into small pieces and add to the batter. Pour a ladleful of batter into a skillet with a shallow layer of grease that has reached 375 degrees. Fry for 3 minutes or till the edges are crispy. Turn over once. Let 'em fry for 3 more minutes and then drain on a paper towel. Sprinkle with powdered sugar.

—*RUBY ANN BOXCAR, LOT #18*

## BATTER CRUST COBBLER

*Dora says it's her cobbler that keeps her husband, Ben, from goin' out at night. I'm sure the fact that he's in a wheelchair plays a part, too.*

1 cup flour

2 teaspoons bakin' powder

1/2 cup sugar

3/4 cup milk

1/2 teaspoon salt

1 can of apple, cherry, or peach pie fillin'

Brown sugar

Margarine

Combine the first three ingredients together. Add the milk and salt and stir well. Pour the batter into a well-greased 12 x 12-inch pan. Pour the can of pie filling on top of the batter. Make sure you spread it all over when pourin' it on top of the batter. Sprinkle some brown sugar on top of the fruit and dot with margarine. Bake at 350 degrees. In around an hour the batter will rise to a bubbly crusty top and the fruit fillin' will be on the bottom. Serve with ice cream, milk, or coffee.

*—DORA BEAVER, LOT #7*

## EGG CUSTARD

*This is some of the best egg custard I've ever had. Nellie says her secret is to use eggs that are a day or two away from expirin'. Remember Nellie's old and neither life nor food poisonin' really doesn't mean all that much to her. I recommend fresh eggs.*

1 cup sugar
5 cups milk
8 eggs
1 teaspoon imitation vanilla extract
Nutmeg

Mix sugar and 3 1/2 cups of milk in a pot and heat until the sugar is dissolved. Beat eggs (slightly), and add 1 1/2 cups of milk. Strain into other mixture. Mix and add the imitation vanilla. Pour into 9 x 13-inch glass dish and sprinkle with nutmeg. Set in a pan of water. Cook for 45 minutes at 350 degrees. To keep the pan from turnin' dark, add 2 teaspoons of cream of tarter to the water.

*—NELLIE TINKLE, LOT #4*

## LULU'S EASY DESSERT

*This is a dish your kids or simple-minded seniors can make with you. The best part is how good it is.*

*CRUST:*
1 cup flour
1 cup nuts
1 stick margarine, melted

Mix the flour, nuts, and melted margarine together. Sprinkle it over the bottom of a 9 x 13-inch pan. Bake for 20 minutes at 350 degrees. Set aside to cool.

*FILLIN':*

8 oz. cream cheese

1 cup powdered sugar

1/2 package whipped cream

Mix all together and spread over the cooled crust.

*TOPPIN':*

3 cups milk

1 package vanilla instant puddin'

1 package chocolate instant puddin'

Mix well and spread over the fillin'. If you've got any whipped cream left over go ahead and put it on top of the toppin'.

—*LULU BOXCAR, LOT #8*

## FRUIT SALAD

*This won Ollie the coveted Hairnet Award back in 1967.*

10 cans sweetened condensed milk (1 can) (recipe is in the COOKIE section)

10 tubs whipped cream (1 tub)

120 oz. pineapple, crushed and drained (12 oz.)

30 bananas, mashed (3)

5 cups nuts, chopped (1/2 cup)

Blend together the milk and whipped cream. Add the pineapple, bananas, and nuts. Stir well. Chill for 2 hours before servin'.

—*OLLIE WHITE, LOT #10*

## SAINT PETER AND PAUL PISTACHIO PRAYER SALAD

*If Sister Bertha had been around durin' our Savior's time, I have no doubt that he'd have fed the multitude with her pistachio salad instead of fishes and loaves.*

9 oz. whipped cream
1 box instant pistachio puddin' mix
1/2 cup small marshmallows
1/2 cup nuts, chopped
1 small can pineapples, crushed and drained
1/2 cup maraschino cherries, chopped
Mix all together and chill for 1 hour.

—*SISTER BERTHA, LOT #12*

## RC COLA SALAD

*This is a little too sweet for me, but it always goes fast at our residents' July 4th gatherin' by the trailer park pool.*

1 can Bing cherries
1 cup water
2 cans RC COLA
2 packages Black Cherry JELL-O
8 oz. pineapple, crushed
1 cup chopped nuts
Place cherries, water, and cola in a cookin' pot and boil for a few minutes. Pour over the JELL-O. When it's cool, add the pineapple and nuts. Put it in the fridge until it sets.

—*ANITA BIGGON, LOT #2*

## DONNA SUE'S RED HOT MOMMA

*It's amazin' what kind of tasty treats a hungry drunk can come up with.*

2/3 cup RED HOTS
1 cup boilin' water
1 box cherry JELL-O
1 can applesauce

Dissolve RED HOTS in the boilin' water. Reheat the water if needed to dissolve the JELL-O. Allow the JELL-O to cool then add the applesauce. Chill in the fridge.

*—DONNA SUE BOXCAR, LOT #6*

## BREAD PUDDIN'

*This is great even without a lemon sauce.*

2 cups dry bread crumbs
4 cups milk, scalded
2 eggs
1/2 cup sugar
1/4 teaspoon salt
1/4 teaspoon nutmeg
1/2 cup raisins
1 teaspoon imitation vanilla extract

Soak bread crumbs in milk until they're soft. Beat the eggs until they're light. Add the sugar, salt, nutmeg, raisins, and imitation vanilla. Mix thoroughly with the bread mixture. Pour into a greased pan and set in a larger pan of hot water. Bake at 350 degrees for 1 hour.

*—MOMMA BALLZAK, LOT #16*

## GRAHAM CRACKER PUDDIN'

*I know it's amazin', but this recipe doesn't call for
any soda pop!*

5 eggs
2 cups sugar
2 cups graham cracker crumbs
2 teaspoons bakin' powder
1 teaspoon imitation vanilla extract
1 cup nuts

Beat eggs and add sugar, crumbs, and other ingredients. Bake at 350 degrees for 30 minutes. Cool and serve with whipped cream.

—*KITTY CHITWOOD, LOT #11*

## RUBY ANN BOXCAR'S DIRT BAG PUDDIN'

*As mentioned in the introduction.*

1/2 cup flour
4 tablespoons instant chocolate drink mix
1/4 cup and 1/3 cup sugar
3/4 teaspoon bakin' powder
1/4 cup milk
1 tablespoon oil
1/2 teaspoon imitation vanilla extract
1/4 cup chocolate wafers, crumbled (recipe is in the COOKIE section)
3/4 cup boilin' water

Stir together the flour, 1 tablespoon of chocolate drink mix, 1/4 cup of sugar, and the bakin' powder. Add the milk, oil, and vanilla, and stir it until it's smooth. Add the wafers, and put it in a pan. Combine the remaining sugar and drink mix, and gradually add the boilin' water. Stir it well, and pour it over the mixture that's already in the pan. Bake it at 350 degrees for 30 minutes. Serve it warm or cold.

—*RUBY ANN BOXCAR, LOT #18*

# DR PEPPER SALAD

*If I hadn't showed up when I did, Connie would've
had Dew sign us up to be Amway distributors just
so he could get a servin' of this dish!*

2 cans DR PEPPER
1 large package cherry JELL-O
1/2 cup maraschino cherries (chopped)
1 small package cream cheese

In a pan heat up 1 can of DR PEPPER over medium heat. When it gets
hot, add JELL-O to the soda.

In a small bowl stir the cherries and cream cheese together. Add it to the
hot JELL-O/DR PEPPER mixture and stir well. Add the other can of
DR PEPPER, pour into a mold, and refrigerate until firm.

—*CONNIE KAY, LOT #13*

# HOMEMADE STRAWBERRY SHORTCAKE

*I put the strawberry shortcake, as shown on the
cover, in the dessert section since it ain't really
a cake.*

1 quart fresh strawberries
1 1/2 cups sugar
2 1/4 cups flour
2 tablespoons sugar
1 tablespoon bakin' powder
Pinch salt
1/2 cup CRISCO
1 egg, beaten
3/4 cup milk
1/2 cup strawberry jam
2 cups whippin' cream, whipped

Put aside one strawberry, and slice up the rest. Put 5 slices aside, and
sweeten the other slices with sugar to taste (I use a cup of sugar).

Combine the flour, 2 tablespoons of sugar, bakin' powder, and salt. Put in the CRISCO and blend with a mixer for 5 minutes. Make a hole in the middle of the mix, and add the egg and milk, which you've already combined. Mix it together with a fork. Lightly flour a surface and put the dough on it. Shape it into a ball and knead lightly for 5 minutes. Divide dough into thirds and put into separate greased round 8-inch cake pans with wax paper in the bottom. Make sure they are evenly spread out to cover the bottom of each pan. Brush the tops with milk and bake at 425 degrees until lightly brown (15–18 minutes). With a dull knife, loosen the edges from the sides of the pans. Remove the cakes from the pans and pull off the wax paper. After the cakes have cooled, spread the jam on two of the tops. Put one of the jammed covered cakes on a plate. Put 1/2 the sweetened sliced strawberries on the cake and some of the whipped cream on the strawberries. Put the second cake on top, add the strawberries and some more whipped cream. The third cake goes on this. Place remainin' whippin' cream in the center of the cake. Add the whole strawberry to the middle of the whippin' cream and carefully place the five slices around it.

—*RUBY ANN BOXCAR, LOT #18*

# Chapter 11

Nellie and C. M. Tinkle of lot #4 are always ready with a helpful hint.

# *Helpful Hints*

Everybody in a trailer park always has some kind of helpful hints. For some reason they've all come up with little tidbits that they feel make life a lot easier. Regardless of what the problem might be, they've got a solution. For example, the first time I had to go on the road for a long period of time was durin' one of the hottest months in the history of Arkansas. I was afraid that my plants would just burn right up in the sun. I really didn't want to bother my family or friends by askin' 'em to come over and water my plants everyday (I knew they wouldn't have anyhow). So I simply let everybody know my situation and in 15 minutes time I had 12 helpful hints. And the best part was that all 12 helpful hints worked!

So here are some hints from the residents of my trailer park. They've passed 'em on to me, and now I can pass 'em on to you. You'll find helpful little ditties for cookin', cleanin', keepin' safe, and just gettin' through life. Plus I've added a weights and measurement chart along with an equivalent chart. Just remember: Pass 'em on to somebody else.

NOTE: I didn't include any of my dear old warped-minded Me-Ma's helpful hints. She gave me a page full, but after readin' 'em I quickly decided against 'em. I didn't want to confuse any of you readers with these bizarre tidbits that she submitted to me. I was afraid that some of you might believe that puttin' a sick poodle in the freezer for one hour might just make it better. I didn't want any of you sendin' me hate letters from the hospital sayin' how you took my Me-Ma's advice and applied gasoline to your inner thighs in an attempt to kill jock itch! So don't worry about the other hints in this section, 'cause I've checked 'em, and they won't hurt you or your family pets. And yes, I'm goin' to black out this section of the book that I give to my Me-Ma.

# EQUIVALENTS

*1 pound of margarine or butter* .......................................................*2 cups*
*2 cups of sugar* .........................................................................*1 pound*
*2 1/2 cups packed brown sugar* ................................................*1 pound*
*3 1/2 cups powdered sugar* .......................................................*1 pound*
*4 cups all-purpose flour* ..........................................................*1 pound*

# WEIGHTS AND MEASUREMENTS

3 teaspoons=1 tablespoon
2 tablespoons=1 fluid ounce
4 tablespoons=1/4 cup
8 tablespoons=1/2 cup
1 cup=1/2 pint
2 cups=1 pint
4 cups=1 quart

# AND NOW FOR THE HELPFUL HINTS!

- If you run out of filters for a coffee maker, paper towels or a single knee-high nylon will make a great substitute.
- Children can carry pictures and papers to school without tearin' 'em if you roll the items and insert 'em in discarded cardboard tubes from wax paper.
- If sugar is put in a large salt shaker it is easier to put on cereal or oatmeal without spillin' it all over the place.
- Semi truck and car radiator valves can be unclogged and cleaned by boiling 'em in vinegar for about 5 minutes. When they're cool enough to handle, slosh 'em around in the coolin' vinegar, rinse well in clear water, and then dry 'em. This will clear the air holes and remove any accumulated particles from inside the valves.

- Crayon marks can be removed by placin' the stained area between clean paper towels or pieces of a brown paper bag and pressing with a warm iron.

- Children are little angels God has sent from heaven for our pleasure.

- To make any day-old food item springy and fresh, pop it into the microwave with a cup of water.

- Addin' bread crumbs to scrambled eggs before cookin' 'em not only improves the flavor, but it makes a larger servin'.

- Refresh stale chips, crackers, or other like snacks by puttin' a plateful in the microwave for 30–45 seconds. Wait 1 minute to crisp.
  —*TAMMY CANTRELL, LOT #1*

- When a recipe calls for creamin' margarine and sugar together, add a little bit of the liquid called for in the ingredients. This will help it cream faster and helps it not to stick to the bowl.

- You won't have any trouble gettin' dumplin' batter to drop from a spoon if you dip the spoon in the boilin' liquid before scoopin' out the batter.

- If sour cream is needed for a recipe, add one tablespoon of vinegar to each cup of cream.

- Use peanut butter to remove the price tags stuck on things.

- To make bread dough rise faster, preheat your oven at its lowest possible settin' for 10 minutes. Turn the oven off. Put the covered mixin' bowl of dough in the oven. It will rise quicker than normal.

- A good honest man is nice, but an old drunk with a bankroll is better.

- Take a minute to stop and smell the roses, but watch out for the pricks.

- If you put potatoes in hot water 15 minutes before bakin' in the oven, it'll only take half the time to cook 'em.

- If you oversalt vegetables or soups, add a few cut raw potatoes and just discard them once they've cooked. They will absorb the salt.
  —*ANITA BIGGON, LOT #2*

- Addin' a bit of instant coffee straight from the jar can brown pale gravy. And don't worry, it won't give you a bitter taste neither.

- Lettuce and celery keep longer if you store 'em in paper bags instead of plastic.

- Always thaw frozen fish out in milk. The milk draws out the frozen taste and provides a fresh-caught flavor.

- Never put oil, margarine, or grease in a cold fryin' pan. Heat the pan, and then add the grease. You will never have anything stick when you do this.

- You can cut a meringue pie cleanly by coatin' both sides of the knife lightly with margarine.

- Puttin' razor blades in an old aspirin box will protect you from accidental cuts.

- Runnin' a drawstring through the hem of your picnic tablecloth will hold it on the table.

- A pie crust will be easier to make if all ingredients are cool.

- Pie crust won't be hard or tough when milk is used in place of the water.

- Before gratin' cheese, brush cookin' oil on the grater. It'll clean up a lot easier.
  —*LOIS BUNCH, LOT #3*

- To eliminate the fat from soup and stew, drop a few ice cubes into the pot and stir. The fat will cling to the cubes. Simply discard the cubes before they melt. You can also wrap the ice cubes in a paper towel and skim it over the top.

- When makin' a fruit pie, put lower crust in the oven and bake for 5 minutes. When you put the fillin' in and cook, your bottom pie crust won't be soggy.

- Do not grease the sides of a cake pan. How would you like to climb a greased pole?

- Use small juice cans that you've cut both the ends off of for cookie cutters. Before liftin' the cutter from the cookie dough, sprinkle through with sugar, nuts, or candies the top of the can to avoid waste and spills.

- Before measurin' syrup, honey, or molasses, grease the measurin' cups or spoons thoroughly with margarine to prevent the syrup from clingin' to the cup or spoon.

- A good and cheap way of destroyin' odors is by burnin' orange peelin's.

- A good use for odds and ends of candles is to melt 'em down over low heat in a pot. Add your favorite spices or cloves and pour into a mold. Add a wick and use as air freshenin'.

- To avoid lumps in bread batter, add a pinch of salt to the flour before it's wet.

- A small dish of water in the oven while bakin' bread will keep it from gettin' a hard crust.

- If you oversweeten a dish, add salt.

- If you oversalted a dish, simply add one teaspoon of cider vinegar and one teaspoon of sugar to remedy the situation.

  *—NELLIE TINKLE, LOT #4*

- Brown sugar won't harden if you place an apple slice or a fresh heel from a loaf of bread in the container.

- To determine whether an egg is fresh, put it in a pan of cool salted water. If it sinks, use it, and if it rises to the surface, CAREFULLY throw it away.

- Use the circular cardboard from the bottom of frozen pizzas when transportin' a cake. Cover with foil first.

- When frostin' a cake, place strips of wax paper beneath the edges of the cake. They can easily be removed after you've finished frostin'.

- When buyin' grapefruit, judge it by its weight. The heavier ones are juicier.

- Perk up soggy lettuce by addin' lemon juice to a bowl of cold water and soak it for an hour in the fridge.
  
  *—MOMMA BOXCAR, LOT #5*

- To open the screw tops on a liquor or beer bottle without any fuss, unscrew 'em with a nutcracker.

- Touch up the keyhole on your trailer's front door with a little luminous paint, and you won't fumble for the lock in the dark.

- Paintin' the lower stair on your trailer steps white will help you find 'em at night.

- If you paint your driveway orange it will make it easier to find where you live at night.

- Touch up the toilet seat with luminous paint and you'll find it easier durin' the middle of the night.

- Put a little luminous paint on the tops of your liquor bottles, and you won't have any problems findin' them durin' the night.

- Men's sex organs are like cars; a Yugo will get you to town, but a stretch limousine makes the trip worthwhile!
  
  *—DONNA SUE BOXCAR, LOT #6*

- You can scald milk in the microwave by cookin' it on high for 2 1/2 minutes, stirrin' after each minute.

- Let raw potatoes stand in the cold water before fryin' to improve their crispness.

- Before boilin' potatoes, rice, or pasta rub margarine around the top inside of the pot to keep 'em from boilin' over.

- Do one good deed each day, and give a smile away.

- You can tell if an egg is hard-boiled by spinnin' it. If it spins, it's hard boiled, but if it wobbles or doesn't spin, it ain't.

- When a drain is clogged with grease, pour a cup of salt and a cup of bakin' soda down the drain followed by a kettle of boilin' water.

    *—DORA BEAVER, LOT #7*

- Puttin' a rib of celery in your bread wrapper will help keep the bread fresh for a longer time.

- Always fill your ice trays with hot water. They will turn to ice faster than cold water will.

- When boilin' water, use cold water in a pot, not hot water. Cold water will boil faster.

- Billy Ray Cyrus rocks!!!

    *—LULU BELL BOXCAR, LOT #8*

- Sprinkle applesauce or banana cake generously with granulated sugar before bakin' to give it a crunchy toppin'.

- Drinkin' and bowlin' don't mix.

- To remove corn silk, just dampen a paper towel and brush downward on the cob of corn.

- Fresh tomatoes keep longer if stored in the refrigerator. Just place 'em so the stems point down.

    *—JUANITA HIX, LOT #9*

- A teaspoon of vinegar added to pie dough helps make a flaky crust.

- A little vinegar rubbed on your fingers will remove the odor of onions from 'em quickly.

- Vinegar will remove fruit stains from your hands.

- If you soak garments in warm vinegar water, you can remove perspiration stains.

- Puttin' a little vinegar in a pot of water when boilin' eggs will stop a cracked egg from leakin' into the water.

- Also when boilin' eggs, pour off the hot water, crack the eggs, and cover 'em with cold water. They will peel much easier.
- Place a bowl of vinegar on the stove when cookin' fish to absorb the smell.

*—OLLIE WHITE, LOT #10*

- When a recipe calls for dry breadcrumbs and you ain't got any, use cereal or potato flakes.
- Roll fruits and raisins in flour before addin' 'em to the cake batter so they'll stay distributed throughout the cake.
- When addin' dry and wet ingredients, begin and end with the dry ingredients, beatin' well after each addition for a smoother batter.

*—KITTY CHITWOOD, LOT #11*

- A prayer a day will keep the devil away.
- If our savior could carry his cross without my help, then so can you.
- If your kids are angels like you say they are then tell 'em to fly over my yard instead of runnin' through it.
- Durin' the wintertime you need to have a homemade emergency kit in your car or truck. Take a small box and put in the followin': an empty 2-lb. coffee can, 1 roll of toilet paper, and a bottle of rubbin' alcohol. If your car should break down durin' really bad weather you can put the toilet paper in the coffee can and pour the alcohol over the toilet paper. Ignite the toilet paper, and roll the window down slightly to let the smoke get out of the car. This will provide up to 8 hours of heat and could save your life.
- One teaspoon of vinegar in the doughnut lard will keep the doughnuts from soakin' up the lard.

*—SISTER BERTHA, LOT #12*

- Biscuits can easily be cut and formed by simply usin' the divider from one of those old metal ice trays. Simply shape the dough to conform with the size of the ice tray divider. Place the divider deep down in the dough and then pull it back out. When the biscuits are baked they'll separate at the dividin' lines.

- When meltin' chocolate, grease the pot first.

- Use a thread or dental floss rather than a knife to cut a hot cake.

- Soak peeled apples in cold water to which 1 teaspoon of salt has been added. They will not discolor.

- When your recipe calls for one cup of sugar and you don't have any in the trailer, substitute 3/4 cup of honey. If you use honey make sure you reduce the total amount of other liquids by 1/4 cup, and reduce bakin' temperature 25 degrees to prevent overbrownin'.

> *—CONNIE KAY, LOT #13*
>
> *—WANDA KAY, LOT #13*

- To prevent soggy crust on a cream pie, simply sprinkle the crust with some powdered sugar.

- Foldin' the top crust over the lower crust before crimpin' will keep the juices in the pie.

- Put aluminum foil over the edges of pie crust to prevent 'em from burnin'.

- Lemons that are heated before squeezin' will give almost twice as much juice.

> *—DOTTIE LAMB, LOT #14*
>
> *—OPAL LAMB, LOT #14*

- Sprinkle a dash of cologne on the bag of your vacuum cleaner and as you vacuum the odor will fill the trailer with a delightful aroma.

- To thread a needle easily, cut thread on a slant.

- An empty milk carton stuffed with newspaper makes an excellent starter for fires in the fireplace. Just punch holes in all the sides and light.

- Add some confectioner's sugar to whippin' cream before beatin'. It'll make it stand up even if it ain't used immediately.
- Put a layer of marshmallows in the bottom of a pumpkin pie, then add the fillin'. You'll have a nice toppin' as they come to the surface.
- Meringue on a pie will be higher if you add a pinch of cream of tartar to the beaten egg whites.
- Be proud of who you are. After all, God is.

*—DONNY OWENS, LOT #15*

*—KENNY LYNN, LOT #15*

- Next time you clean your blender, fill it halfway up with hot water and a teaspoon of your favorite dishwashin' detergent. Before you turn your blender on, drop in a couple of ice cubes. When the blender's on, they will dislodge pieces of food that are stuck to the sides.
- Don't add salt to a lettuce salad until just before servin', 'cause salt makes the lettuce wilt and become tough.
- Booze is God's answer to mirrors.

*—MOMMA BALLZAK, LOT #16*

- When you've got to tie somethin' up real good, and you don't have any rope, duct tape works great.
- Make sure you always have a back-up plan just in case your original plan goes wrong.
- Batteries stored in the freezer last longer and stay fresh until you need 'em.
- If you want to write somethin' that no one else should read, write it on flash paper with lemon juice. You can read the blank lookin' paper by holdin' it up to a light. When you're done with it, just light the flash paper and it'll burn right up without a trace.
- You can use plastic bags on your hands when you don't want to leave fingerprints on things.

*—MABLE SCAGGS, LOT #17*

- Put a song in your heart, and you'll have a smile everyday.
- Love your neighbor, not their husband.
- To keep chocolate cakes brown on the outside, dust the greased pan with cocoa instead of flour.
- Store chocolate in a dry place. Chocolate that has been exposed to moisture won't melt properly.
- Before heatin' milk in a pot, rinse the pot with cold water. It will prevent stickin'.
- A wedge of lemon cooked with onion or cabbage will absorb the cookin' odors.
- Let a cake set on a rack for 5 minutes before tryin' to take it out of the pan.
- Only frost a cake that has completely cooled.

*—RUBY ANN BOXCAR, LOT #18*

- An easy way to make the right-size hamburger buns is to grease a large fruit juice can (46-oz.) and fill it one-third full of bread dough. When baked, this loaf will store more easily than buns and can be cut into tasty slices that are just the right size.
- When a recipe calls for an egg and you ain't got any, use 1/2 cup of mayonnaise instead.
- When thawin' frozen fruit, put it in some water. It will keep the fruit from turnin' dark.

*—JEANNIE JANSSEN, LOT #19*

- If God would've meant for us to be Republicans, our brains would be the size of our eyeballs.
- Love is like a rotten egg. If you don't handle it with care, it'll stink your house up.
- Nuts will come out of the shell in halves if soaked overnight in salt water before crackin'. After you crack black walnuts, let 'em set overnight and they can be removed from the shell easier.

- Keep unpopped popcorn in the freezer to help eliminate unpopped kernels.

- Sprinkle popcorn lightly with warm water and let stand a few hours before poppin'. The added moisture makes it pop better.

- Slip plastic bags onto your hands when shapin' popcorn balls to avoid stickin' and burns.

- If you don't vote on election day, you can't complain about it the next day.

—*LOVIE BIRCH, LOT #20*

# Chapter 12

Marty Scaggs's new wife, Mable, standin' in front of a photo of
the late Eula Scaggs, of lot #17 is as close to low fat as you get in a trailer park.

# *Low Fat*

The closest thing you'll find to low fat in a trailer park is a bowl of ice cream without any hot fudge on it. We don't believe in that calorie countin' kind of eatin'. It's like I told Richard Simmons when we were in the green room at the "Late Night With David Letterman Show," "If God had meant for me to be thin, He would've given me a high metabolism." If our creator saw fit to give us all these foods that look and taste good, who are we to say "I can't eat that." So if you're lookin' for low-fat recipes, you've bought the wrong damn book!

# Chapter 13

Lois and Hubert Bunch of lot #3 stops 'em dead in their tracks
with their **Tostada De Lois**.

# Main Dishes

The main dish is just that, the main dish at a meal. It doesn't really matter what it consists of or what style it is just as long as it has some kind of meat in it. Trust me when I say, you won't find a vegetarian livin' in a trailer park. They wouldn't last 10 minutes once their dirty little eatin' secret got out! It's like Pastor Hickey preached one Sunday, "Eatin' a non-meat dish just ain't Christian! God gave us these animals to eat, and if you don't eat 'em, you're slappin' God in the face!" Usually the meat is beef or pork or a mixture of both in a processed form. Even though we like chicken, it tends to be a little pricey, but I've included some of our favorite chicken dishes, too. So get your pots, pans, skillets, and casserole dishes out, 'cause it's time to cook some good eatin's!

## ALL-DAY CROCK POT DELIGHT

*Yet another beer recipe from Kitty.*

Serves 4
2–3 lb. roast, cut into cubes
1/2 cup flour
1/4 cup margarine
1 onion, sliced
1 teaspoon salt
1/8 teaspoon pepper
1 clove garlic, minced
2 cups beer
1/4 cup flour

A little water

Cooked rice

Coat beef cubes with 1/2 cup of flour. Brown in melted margarine. Drain off the excess fat. In a crock pot, combine browned meat with onion, salt, pepper, garlic, and beer. Cover and cook on low for 5 to 7 hours until the meat is tender. Turn control to high, and dissolve the remainin' 1/4 cup of flour in a small amount of water. Stir into the crock pot mixture. Cook on high for 30 to 40 minutes. Serve as is or with rice.

—*KITTY CHITWOOD, LOT #11*

## SOUTH OF THE BORDER BEEF SKILLET LA LOIS

*The whole trailer park smells like cheap Mexican food when Lois cooks up a batch of this. Needless to say, we all come up with some reason to drop by her trailer durin' dinnertime.*

*Serves 4*

1 lb. ground beef

1 tablespoon oil

1/4 cup onion, diced

2 teaspoons salt

1 teaspoon chili powder

1/4 teaspoon pepper

1 lb. tomatoes

1 can whole kernel corn

1 bouillon cube dissolved in 1 1/4 cup water

1/2 cup thin strips green bell pepper

1 1/3 cups minute rice

Put the meat in a skillet, and brown the meat in oil at a high heat. Leave the meat in coarse chunks. Add onions, reduce heat to medium, and cook until the onions are tender (not browned). Add seasonin', tomatoes, corn, and bouillon. Bring to a boil. Stir in green pepper. Boil again. Stir in rice, remove from the heat, cover, and let stand for 5 minutes. Fluff it up with a fork and serve.

—*LOIS BUNCH, LOT #3*

# TRAILER PARK GOULASH

*This stuff will have 'em beggin' for more! And here's a little secret for those of you that have to feed a large family: Just add another pound or two of beef and another jar of sauce to stretch it out even more.*

*Serves 4 to 5*

1 tablespoon margarine
2 lbs. ground beef
Large onion
1 teaspoon salt
1 cup tomatoes, strained
1 jar spaghetti sauce
1 bag elbow or shell noodles
1 can corn

Put the margarine in a skillet and brown the meat and the onion. Season with salt, and add both the tomatoes and the jar of spaghetti sauce. Cover and cook on low for 1 hour. Follow the instructions on the bag of noodles to get 'em going. When the noodles are finished, drain off the water and add the can of corn. Stir in the meat mixture. Serve as is or with a slice of cheese on top.

—*JEANNIE JANSSEN, LOT #19*

## ARKANSAS HASH

*Anita came up with this hash recipe durin' one of
her bouts with depression in Fort Smith.*

Serves 6 to 8

3 large onions, thinly sliced
1 large green pepper, minced
3 tablespoons margarine
2 lbs. ground beef
4 cups tomatoes, cooked
1/2 cup uncooked rice
2 teaspoons chili powder
2 teaspoons salt
1/8 teaspoon pepper
1/2 cup vodka
1/2 cup rum
1/2 cup gin

Sauté onions and green pepper in margarine until tender. Add meat and brown it until crumbly. Stir in remainin' ingredients, and pour into a greased bakin' dish. Cover and bake at 350 degrees for 45 minutes. Remove the cover and bake for 15 more minutes. When servin', make sure to use bowls so everybody gets a lot of the juices that come with each spoonful. Serve with bread.

—*ANITA BIGGON, LOT #2*

## MOMMA BALLZAK'S POOR GAL DINNER

*Momma Ballzak recommends a red wine with
this meal. She also says if you ain't got any red
wine then go ahead and use a white wine. If you
ain't got any wine then drink whatever you've got
in the house!*

*Serves 4 to 14*
3 lbs. hamburger
4 large carrots, grated
1 onion, grated
2 potatoes, grated
2 eggs
1 teaspoon garlic, minced
1 tablespoon salt
Pepper to taste
14 slices bacon

Mix beef, carrots, onion, potatoes, eggs, garlic, salt, and pepper together. Form into 14 patties and wrap a slice of bacon around each of 'em. If you need to, secure the bacon to the patty with a toothpick. Broil to desired doneness. Take out the toothpick and serve as is.

—*MOMMA BALLZAK, LOT #16*

# DONNA SUE'S CHEESY HAMBURGER DISH

*This is a great dish to make when you're trying to beat the clock. It's fast and easy, just like my sister, Donna Sue.*

*Serves 4 to 6*
1 lb. hamburger
Salt
Pepper
A-1 sauce
Government cheese
1 can cream of celery soup

Place the uncooked hamburger meat in a layer in a bakin' dish. Sprinkle with salt, pepper, and A-1 sauce. Cover it with cheese. Pour the soup over the cheese. Cover and bake at 350 degrees for 45 minutes. This is also great with cream of mushroom soup!

—*DONNA SUE BOXCAR, LOT #6*

## MOMMA'S MEAT LOAF

*This is Daddy's favorite dish. When Momma served meat loaf we knew that she'd either spent too much money while shoppin' or she was "in the mood."*

*Serves 5 to 8*

1 1/2 lbs. ground beef

2 eggs

1 cup crushed cornflakes

1 onion, diced

1/2 bell pepper, diced

3/4 teaspoon salt

Pepper to taste

1 small can tomato sauce

Combine all the ingredients together and form into a loaf.

*TOPPIN':*

6 tablespoons brown sugar

1 can tomato soup

1 cup ketchup

1 tablespoon Worcestershire sauce

Mix together and pour over the loaf. Cook for an hour and a half at 350 degrees.

—*MOMMA BOXCAR, LOT #5*

## LITTLE TOWN OF BETHLEHEM BAKED BEANS

*This little bean dish has become a tradition at the Christmas feedin' I spoke of earlier. Some have even said this is what makes the Lutherans come back every year.*

*Serves 8 to 10*

1 lb. hamburger meat

1/2 cup onion, finely chopped

1/4 cup green sweet pepper, chopped

1/2 cup celery, sliced

8 oz. tomato sauce

1/2 cup water

1 tablespoon vinegar

1 clove garlic, minced or mashed

1 teaspoon dry mustard

1/2 teaspoon thyme

1 tablespoon brown sugar

1-lb. can pork and beans

Salt and pepper to taste

Cook the hamburger, and don't drain. Add onion, green pepper, and celery. Sauté until the beef is brown, and the veggies are limp. Stir the remainin' ingredients other than the beans into the meat mixture, and simmer together for 5 minutes. Empty the beans into a large bakin' dish and spoon meat mixture over the top. Bake at 375 degrees for 45 minutes.

—*SISTER BERTHA, LOT #12*

# CHIHUAHUAS

*Just like Lois serves at the Taco Tackle Shack minus the smell of the stink bait!*

Serves 10

10 hot dog buns, toasted

6 oz. corn chips

10 hot dogs, grilled

1 lb. chili

1/2 head lettuce, shredded

1/4 lb. Government cheese

Line the buns with the chips. Add the hot dogs, and top with a large spoonful of chili, lettuce, and cheese.

—*LOIS BUNCH, LOT #3*

## SOUR CREAM NOODLE BAKE

*When I'm comin' over to eat, Dora always knows
to make a double batch of this noodle delight.*

Serves 4 to 6

8 oz. noodles
1 lb. ground beef
1 tablespoon margarine
1 teaspoon salt
1/8 teaspoon pepper
1/4 teaspoon garlic salt
1 can tomato sauce
1 cup sour cream
1 cup cottage cheese
8 green onions, chopped
1 cup Government cheese, shredded

Cook the noodles accordin' to the package. Rinse and drain. Brown the meat in the margarine, and add salt, pepper, garlic salt, and tomato sauce. Simmer for 5 minutes. Combine the sour cream, cottage cheese, and green onions. In a bakin' dish put a layer of noodles, layer of meat mixture, layer of sour cream mixture, and a layer of cheese. Continue layerin' until the dish is full. Make sure you've got some cheese on the top. Bake at 350 degrees for 25 to 30 minutes.

—*DORA BEAVER, LOT #7*

## SKILLET SPAGHETTI

*This is a great dish for those of you that have a lot
of kids, and only a little time to cook.*

Serves 6 to 8

1 tablespoon shortenin'
1 lb. ground beef
3/4 cup onion, chopped

1/2 cup green peppers, chopped
1 clove garlic, minced
2 teaspoons salt
4 cups water
1/2 lb. spaghetti, broken into 2-inch pieces
1 lb. tomatoes, cut into bite-size pieces
3/4 cup ketchup

Put the shortenin' in a large deep skillet. Brown the next 4 ingredients. Sprinkle with salt, and stir in the water. Bring the mixture to a boil, and add the spaghetti. Cook uncovered for 15 minutes or until the spaghetti is tender. Stir in tomatoes and ketchup. Simmer for 10 minutes. Serve with parmesan cheese.

*—TAMMY CANTRELL, LOT #1*

## SLOPPY SLOPPY-JOES

*Trust me when I tell you if you serve this dish, you'll want to cover your table with plastic trash bags first! This stuff lives up to its name!*

Serves 6
1 lb. ground beef
1 onion, finely chopped
1/4 cup green pepper, chopped
1 clove garlic
1 can tomato soup
1 can corn
1 beef bouillon cube dissolved in 1/2 cup boilin' water
Salt and pepper to taste

In a skillet brown the beef, drain the excess fat, and add the onion, green pepper, and garlic. Cook for 5 minutes or until the veggies are tender. Stir in the soup, corn, and bouillon. Bring the mixture to a boil and simmer for 10 minutes. Add the salt and pepper. Serve on a bun.

*—JUANITA HIX, LOT #9*

## TIPPER TATOR TOT CASSEROLE

*Lovie told me that every time Al Gore visits, he requests this dish, which is why she named it after Tipper.*

Serves 4 to 6
1 lb. ground beef
2 tablespoons onion, minced
1 can cream of chicken soup
1 can cheddar cheese soup
2 cups Government cheese, shredded
20 tater tots

Brown the meat in skillet and add the onion. Cook for 1 minute. In a casserole dish, combine half the meat mixture and the cream of chicken soup. Add the remainin' meat mixture and top with the cheddar cheese soup. Sprinkle the shredded cheese on top of the mixture. Cover it with the tater tots and bake at 350 degrees for 1 hour.

—*LOVIE BIRCH, LOT #20*

## ENCHILADA CASSEROLE

*Gas, gas, gas, but good, good, good!*

Serves 10 to 12
3 lbs. ground beef
1 green bell pepper, chopped
2 tablespoons chili powder
Water
1 can cream of mushroom soup
2 cans enchilada sauce
1 can green chilies, chopped and drained
1 cup Government cheese, grated

Blend the first three ingredients together and cook until the meat is brown. Drain and add cream of mushroom soup, 1/2 soup can of water, enchilada sauce, chopped green chilies, and cheese to the meat mixture. Mix well. Layer tortillas with the meat mixture and cheese. Roll the tortillas up and place 'em in a bakin' pan. Put remainin' cheese on top of the rolled tortillas and pour some enchilada sauce on 'em. Bake at 350 degrees for 1 hour.

*—LOIS BUNCH, LOT #3*

## OLLIE'S CHICKEN POT PIE

*I'm not a real big chicken eater, but I can always find it in my heart to eat this.*

Serves 4 to 8
1/2 cup margarine, melted
3 tablespoons flour
3 cups chicken broth
1 cup milk
3 cups cooked chicken, diced
1/2 tablespoon salt
1/4 tablespoon pepper
16 oz. mixed veggies, drained
16 oz. green peas, drained
2 9-inch pie crusts

Combine margarine and flour in a pot over low heat. Gradually add the chicken broth and milk. Stir constantly until it's smooth and has thickened. Stir in the chicken, salt, pepper, mixed veggies, and peas. Make sure you mix well. Pour into a 13 x 9 x 2-inch bakin' pan. Put the pie crusts over the top of the pan. Cut slits in the crust. Bake at 350 degrees for 30 minutes or until golden brown.

*—OLLIE WHITE, LOT #10*

# AUNT VIOLET'S SAUSAGE BREAD

*This is my momma's sister. Aunt Violet has always been the black sheep of the family. Not content with the trailer park life, she up and married a Lutheran, and moved to a small town in Illinois. Even though she's converted and lives in a regular house, I still love to cook her sausage bread.*

2 loafs of bread dough, like you find in the freezer section of the grocery store.

3 cups Government cheese, grated

1 lb. sausage, cooked

1 lb. hamburger meat, cooked

1 bell pepper, chopped

1 onion, chopped

Spread one of the thawed loafs out on a bakin' sheet. Sprinkle 1 1/2 cups of cheese on the bread dough. Sprinkle both of the meats on top the cheese. Sprinkle the bell pepper and onion on top of the meat. Sprinkle the remainin' cheese on top. Take the second thawed bread loaf and roll it out until it's big enough to fit on top of the first one. Place it on top and brush it with a light coatin' of margarine. Bake at 350 degrees for 40 to 45 minutes.

*—RUBY ANN BOXCAR, LOT #18*

# NEW YORK CITY REUBEN PIE BAKE

*My Jewish friends in the Big Apple got me hooked on Reuben Sandwiches. I took that love and gave it a trailer park twist so even a good Baptist could enjoy the taste.*

*Serves 4 to 6*

6 slices rye bread

1/4 cup thousand island dressin'

1/2 pound corned beef

8 ounces drained sauerkraut

2 eggs

1/2 cup milk

1 1/2 cups Swiss cheese, shredded

Cut the crust off the bread. Place the bread in a pan you've greased with butter. Make sure the pan's bottom is completely lined with the bread. Spread the Thousand Island Dressin' evenly on the bread. Add the corned beef and spoon the drained sauerkraut on top of the corned beef. Beat the eggs and milk together. Pour the mixture over the sauerkraut. Top with the Swiss cheese and bake at 350 degrees till the cheese bubbles and starts to turn slightly brown. Take it out of the oven and let it cool for 5 minutes. Cut into squares and serve with a pickle.

*—RUBY ANN BOXCAR, LOT #18*

## HUBERT'S FRIED CATFISH

*Hubert and Lois have added this to the Taco Tackle Shack menu even though it ain't Mexican.*

Serves 4

Combine 3/4 cup yellow cornmeal, 1/4 cup flour, 2 teaspoons salt, 1 teaspoon cayenne pepper, 1/4 teaspoon garlic powder in a large bowl (make sure it's large enough for you to dip your fish in).

Coat 4 catfish fillets or whole catfish with the mixture, shakin' off the excess (if you use the frozen fillets, which is just fine, make sure they're thawed out before usin'). Fill a skillet half full with vegetable oil. Heat it to 350-degrees. Add the catfish in a single layer, and fry until it's golden brown. Remove and drain on paper towels. Serve with fries, potato salad, cole slaw, and a big piece of corn bread.

*—HUBERT BUNCH, LOT #3*

## RUBY ANN'S CHICKEN DISH

*Like I said earlier, I don't eat a lot of chicken, but this is one of my favorite chicken dishes. It's simple to make, and it's one of my husband Dew's favorite dishes.*

Serves 8 to 10
1 cup uncooked rice
1 can cream of mushroom soup
1 package LIPTON ONION SOUP MIX
2 cups water
1 cut up chicken

Put the rice in a 9 x 13-inch bakin' dish. Lay pieces of chicken on top of the rice. Mix all the other ingredients together and pour over the chicken and rice. Cook at 350 degrees uncovered for 1 1/2 hours. Cover it up real good and cook for an additional 1/2 hour. Serve as it is.

—*RUBY ANN BOXCAR, LOT #18*

## SPAMRONI

*Finally two of the best types of food have come together to make one darn good food dish.*

Serves 5
1 box macaroni and cheese mix
1 can SPAM sliced
tomato slices
1/2 cup bread crumbs

Fix the macaroni and cheese accordin' to the box instructions. Put the SPAM slices in a casserole dish. Cover with the macaroni and cheese. Put the tomato slices and bread crumbs on top. Bake at 375 degrees for 45 minutes.

—*CONNIE KAY, LOT #13*

## CORNFLAKES TUNA PIE

*Nellie has a blue ribbon to prove how good this
dish tastes.*

Serves 4

2 cups noodles

6 oz. can of tuna

1 can cream of mushroom soup

Cornflakes

Worcestershire sauce

Cook the noodles as directed on the box (feel free to use the noodles of
your choosin'). Drain the tuna and separate with a fork into large flakes.
Grease up a bakin' dish real good and arrange the cooked noodles and tuna
in the dish. Pour the soup over the noodles and tuna. Top with cornflakes,
sprinkle with Worcestershire sauce, and bake at 350 degrees until the top is
brown. Serve with Kitty Chitwood's SLUT PUPPIES.

—*NELLIE TINKLE, LOT #4*

## DOTTIE'S SECRET SWEET-AND-SOUR FISH PIE

*Never tell me that somethin' is secret, so I can't
have the recipe!*

Serves 4

2 cups canned fish

1 egg

1 cup sweet and sour sauce

1/2 teaspoon paprika

2 teaspoons lemon juice

3 tablespoons parsley, minced

2 tablespoons celery, chopped

2 tablespoons onions, chopped

2 tablespoons green pepper, chopped

3/4 cup oriental noodles

Place ingredients (minus noodles) in a large bowl and mix well, makin' sure that the egg mixes with all ingredients. Put in a greased bakin' dish and top with the noodles. Bake for about 30 minutes at 350 degrees.

—*DOTTIE LAMB, LOT #14*

## EULA'S STRING BEAN DELIGHT

*When I was recovin' from havin' my tubes tied, Eula brought me and my husband, Dew, a big bakin' pan of this. Eula was always one to help out those in need or in their sick beds. She was a fine woman. I'm sure Mable will be just as kind and carin'.*

Serves 6

1 lb. hamburger, browned and drained
1 lb. green beans
1 can cream of tomato soup
3 tablespoons horseradish
1/4 teaspoon salt
1/4 teaspoon paprika
1/4 cup Government cheese, grated

Put hamburger and green beans in a greased bakin' dish. Mix tomato soup, horseradish, salt, and paprika together in a bowl. Pour the mixture over beans and hamburger. Top with cheese. Bake at 350 degrees until the cheese is lightly brown. Serve hot from the oven or let it stand for 5 to 10 minutes.

—*MABLE SCAGGS, LOT #17*

## CATFISH FAJITAS

*Lynn said that this is the only fish that he or Donny will eat.*

*Serves 4*

2 lbs. catfish fillets

1 cup lime juice (5–6 limes)

3 cups mesquite or hickory wood chips

1 large onion, sliced and separated into rings

1 large green pepper, cut into strips

2 cloves garlic, minced

2 tablespoons margarine

1/2 teaspoon salt

1/4 teaspoon pepper

8 flour tortillas, warmed

Salsa

Sour cream

Guacamole

Lime wedges

Place the fish in a large plastic bag. Pour lime juice over fish. Seal bag and marinate in refrigerator for one hour ONLY! Soak the wood chips in water for 45 minutes. Drain the wood chips. In a covered grill, test coals for medium-hot heat. Sprinkle wood chips over preheated coals. Lightly brush grill rack with cookin' oil. Place catfish on grill rack. Cover and grill directly over medium-hot coals for 5 minutes on each side or until fish flakes easily. In a large skillet cook onion, green pepper, and garlic in the margarine until they're tender. Stir in the salt and pepper. Cut the grilled catfish into chunks. Toss 'em with the onion mixture. Fill tortillas with the catfish mixture. Serve with salsa, sour cream, guacamole, and lime wedges.

*—DONNY OWENS, LOT #15*

## SWEET POTATO CASSEROLE

*This is great for those nights when you've forgotten to thaw out meat. My husband, Dew, also likes this with pimento loaf sandwiches.*

Serves 4

3 cups mashed sweet potatoes

1 cup sugar

2 eggs

1 teaspoon imitation vanilla extract

1/2 cup orange juice

1/2 cup margarine

Mix all the ingredients together and put in a 9 x 12-inch pan

*TOPPIN':*

1 cup flour

1 cup brown sugar

1/2 cup marshmallows

Mix together and put on the top of the sweet potatoes. Bake for 30 minutes at 350 degrees.

—*TAMMY CANTRELL, LOT #1*

## TACO-RONI SALAD

*I like this dish heated, but Connie says she always serves it cold. Now you serve it how you want, hot or cold, but you might keep in mind that Connie only dusts her trailer once every few months and doesn't like chocolate.*

Serves 5

2 cups uncooked macaroni

1 pound hamburger meat

1 package taco seasonin' mix

1/2 cup French dressin'
1/2 head lettuce, shredded
1 pint cherry tomatoes, halved
1 cup Government cheese, shredded
1/2 cup green onions, chopped

Cook the macaroni accordin' to the package. When done, drain and rinse with cold water. After a second drainin' put it in the fridge so it can chill for one hour. Durin' this time, go ahead and cook the hamburger meat. Crumble the meat in the skillet and then drain off the drippin's. Add the taco seasonin' and French dressin'. Mix well. After the hour has passed take the macaroni out of the fridge, and add it to the meat mixture. Put the meat and macaroni mixture in a large bowl. Add the remainin' ingredients. Toss well. Serve salad immediately.

*—CONNIE KAY, LOT #13*

## TOSTADA DE LOIS

*This dish put the Taco Tackle Shack on the map!*

*Serves 6*
1 pound ground beef
1/2 cup onion (chopped)
1 clove garlic (minced)
1/2 teaspoon salt
1/2 teaspoon chili powder
1 8-oz. can cut green beans
1 8-oz. can red kidney beans
6 10-inch flour tortillas
Cookin' oil
1 large tomato (chopped)
1 small head lettuce (shredded)
1 cup (4 oz.) Government cheese (shredded)
Creamy French salad dressin'

Brown the beef, onion, and garlic in a skillet. Drain off fat. Add 1/2 teaspoon of salt and the chili powder. Stir well and put on low heat to keep it warm.

Combine the undrained green beans and kidney beans; heat and drain. Fry the tortillas one at a time for 20 to 40 seconds in hot cookin' oil until golden brown. Drain on paper towel. Put some meat, beans, tomato, lettuce, and cheese on each fried tortilla. When ready to eat, pour on creamy French salad dressin' to desired amount.

*—LOIS BUNCH, LOT #3*

# Chapter 14

Everybody loves Ben and Dora Beaver of lot #7 almost as much
as they love **Dora's Good as It Gets Pecan Pie.**

# *Pies*

In the olden days, back before the invention of air-conditioners, people in trailer parks would make non-holiday pies durin' the hot times of the year and cakes durin' the colder spells. The reason for this is that most pies are served direct from the refrigerator while nonfrosted cakes are served fresh from the oven. It was a matter of keepin' cool! Today, we make pies and cakes anytime of the year without worryin' about the weather. And when you go to a county or state fair, you'll be surprised at all the pies that are entered for competition. Most of the ribbons my momma has won have been on her pie entries. Needless to say, we just love pies, the baked ones and the nonbaked ones. And after makin' some of these, you will, too!

## MOMMA BOXCAR'S FLAKY PIE CRUST

*If you like a good flaky crust, this is the one.*

*Makes 2 crusts*
1 1/2 cups flour
1/2 cup CRISCO
1/4 teaspoon salt
1/4 cup chilled water

Sift flour and leave 1/4 cup out on board. Mix flour, salt, and CRISCO. Blend until crumbly, then add water. The less you mix the crust the better. Work into a ball with hands then divide into half. Roll into desired pie pan size. Bake at 350 degrees until light brown.

—*MOMMA BOXCAR, LOT #5*

## FRIED PIE CRUST

*This recipe is real handy to make for those of us that hate makin' crust every time we feel like havin' a pie.*

1 cup shortenin'
4 or 5 cups flour
1 egg
1 cup sweetened condensed milk (recipe is in the COOKIE section)
2 teaspoons salt
3 tablespoons sugar (optional)

Mix shortenin' and flour with pastry cutter or fork. Beat egg well then pour in milk, salt, and sugar. Mix well. Pour mixture over flour/shortenin' mix and stir until smooth. This will store in the refrigerator for up to three weeks rolled in plastic wrap. When ready to use, pinch off enough for size pie crust you want to use.

—*OLLIE WHITE, LOT #10*

## PIE CRUST

*This is Dora's award-winnin' pie crust recipe.*

*Makes 3 double crusts*
2 egg yolks
5 cups (all-purpose) flour
4 tablespoons sugar
1/2 teaspoon bakin' powder
1/2 teaspoon salt
1 1/2 cups pure lard

Put egg yolks in a measurin' cup, add enough cold water to fill cup, beat together. Sift all dry ingredients together, and work in the lard. Add the beaten egg yolks and water, store in refrigerator. (Remove from refrigerator and let get almost to room temperature before usin'.)

—*DORA BEAVER, LOT #7*

# TINKLE PIE CRUST

*Nellie always mentions that her pie crust has won both the county and the state fair competitions as well as the Mississippi State Fair back when she and C. M. had their winter trailer in Hattiesburg.*

4 cups unsifted all-purpose flour, lightly spooned into cup
1 tablespoon sugar
2 teaspoons salt
1 3/4 cups solid vegetable shortenin' (not refrigerated)
1/2 cup water
1 tablespoon white or cider vinegar
1 large egg

Put first three ingredients in large bowl and mix well with fork. Add shortenin', and mix well once again usin' a fork until all ingredients are nice and crumbly. Next, in a small bowl, carefully mix together with fork 1/2 cup water, vinegar, and egg. Combine the two mixtures, stirrin' with a fork until all ingredients are moistened. Divide dough in 5 portions with hands. Shape each portion into a flat round patty, ready for rollin'. Wrap in wax paper, chill at least half an hour. Take out and use as needed.

—*NELLIE TINKLE, LOT #4*

# WALDORF ASTORIA PIE CRUST

*Donny and Lynn picked this recipe up durin' one of their antique huntin' trips in New York City. It just amazes me how good both Donny and Lynn can cook. For men, they're quite domestic.*

3/4 cup CRISCO
2 cups flour
1/2 teaspoon salt dissolved in 6–8 tablespoons cold water

Cut shortenin' into flour. Add 6 tablespoons water (use more if needed). The secret of this pie crust is to dissolve salt in the water.

*—DONNY OWENS, LOT #15*

## MARGARITA PIE

*Lois had to get a liquor license just to sell this at the Taco Tackle Shack.*

1 1/2 cups pretzels, finely crushed
8 tablespoons margarine, softened
1 cup and 3 tablespoons sugar
1 envelope unflavored gelatin
1/2 cup lemon juice
4 eggs, separated
1 teaspoon grated lemon rind
1/4 teaspoon salt
5 tablespoons tequila
3 tablespoons Triple Sec
Lemon slices
Lime slices
Pretzel sticks

Grease a 9-inch pie plate. Combine pretzel crumbs, margarine, and 3 tablespoons of sugar in a large bowl until well blended. Press the mixture evenly against the sides and bottom of a prepared pie plate. Let it chill while you sprinkle the gelatin over the lemon juice in a small cup. Let this mixture stand for 5 minutes to soften.

Beat the yolks in the top of a double boiler until foamy. Beat in 1/2 cup sugar. Stir in the lemon rind, salt, and the gelatin/lemon mixture. Cook over simmerin' water, stirrin' constantly, until gelatin is completely dissolved and mixture is thickened slightly (about 8 minutes). Remove from heat, and stir in the Tequila and Triple Sec. Place the pan in a bowl of ice and water, and let it chill while stirrin' often. The mixture is done when it mounds while bein' spooned.

Beat the egg whites in a medium-size bowl until they're foamy. Gradually beat in the remainin' sugar until the meringue forms a soft peak. Fold the meringue until there are no white streaks remainin'. Spoon the mixture into the crust and put it in the fridge to chill for one hour. Garnish it with the lemon and lime slices as well as the pretzel sticks.

*—LOIS BUNCH, LOT #3*

## HONEY MERINGUE

*This meringue can really make a pie special. I even like to eat it on top of vanilla puddin'.*

2 egg whites
dash of salt
1 cup honey

Beat egg whites with salt until stiff enough to hold up in peaks, but not dry. Pour honey in fine stream over egg whites, beatin' constantly, about 10 to 15 minutes or until frostin' holds its shape or beat about 21/2 minutes at the high speed with an electric mixer. This makes a delicious toppin' for any cake or puddin'.

*—WANDA KAY, LOT #13*

## MERINGUE FOR 9-INCH PIE

*Like the name says—perfect for 9-inch pies. Light 'n' fluffy.*

3 egg whites
1/4 teaspoon cream of tartar
6 tablespoons sugar
1/2 teaspoon flavorin', if desired

Mix together and beat until stiff peaks form. Spread on pie and bake at 400 degrees for 8 to 10 minutes.

Note: Remember, bakin' too long and incomplete blendin' of sugar causes "weepin'". For a smooth, clean cut, dip knife into hot water and dry before cuttin' meringue.

—*JUANITA HIXS, LOT #9*

## NEVER FAIL PIE MERINGUE

*It's too bad Tammy can't say this about the elastic in her stretch pants.*

1 tablespoon cornstarch
6 tablespoons sugar
1/2 cup water
Salt (few grains)
3 egg whites

Mix cornstarch, sugar, water, and salt. Cook until thick and clear, stirrin' constantly. Set off the burner. Beat egg whites until they get frothy. Continue beatin', while slowly pourin' the cooked mixture into the egg whites. Beat for 5 minutes. Cover cooled fillin' in a pie shell with meringue, sealin' the edges to the crust. Bake in the 450-degree oven for 5 to 7 minutes.

—*TAMMY CANTRELL, LOT #1*

## CHEESY APPLE PIE

*When Hugh Grant came to stay with me and my husband, Dew, right after the scandal with the hooker, he fell in love with Lulu's pie.*

4 apples
1/2 stick margarine, soft
1/2 cup flour
1/2 cup sugar
1 cup Government cheese, grated

Core and slice apples and spread evenly in bakin' dish. Mix margarine, flour, sugar, and cheese. Press over sliced apples and bake covered for 45 minutes. Uncover and bake until brown. May serve topped with ice cream or whipped cream if desired.

*—LULU BELL BOXCAR, LOT #8*

## ADAM AND EVE'S APPLE FRIED PIES

*In an attempt to discourage the celebration of Halloween, the First Baptist Church of Pangburn held their second annual "Holy Weenie Roast." Sister Bertha handed these little pies out to all the kids that came dressed as characters from the Bible. A good time was had by all—especially at midnight, when Pastor Hickey performed exorcisms on all the children that came dressed as ghosts, devils, or a Teletubbie.*

*Makes 10 to 12 pies*
FILLING:
2 1/2 cups canned apple slices
3/4 cup light brown sugar
1 teaspoon cinnamon
1/2 teaspoon nutmeg
1/4 teaspoon allspice
1 tablespoon flour
1/4 cup seedless raisins
PASTRY:
2 cups flour
2 tablespoons sugar
1/2 teaspoon salt
2/3 cup shortenin'
1/4 cup water (about)
Confectioners sugar

Drain apple slices, then chop fine. Combine apples, brown sugar, cinnamon, nutmeg, allspice, one tablespoon of flour, and raisins. Sift together 2 cups flour, sugar, and salt. Cut in shortenin'. Add enough water to make a firm dough. Roll out dough to 1/8-inch thickness. Cut into 5-inch circles. Place some of the apple mixture on one half of each circle. Moisten edge of pastry with water. Fold over and press edges firmly together with a fork. Fry in deep fat heated to 375 degrees for 31/2 to 4 minutes. Drain on paper towels. Dust with confectioners sugar. If you prefer to bake these crispy apple pies in the oven, bake at 425 degrees for 25 minutes.

*—SISTER BERTHA, LOT #12*

## MOMMA BALLZAK'S APPLE PIE

*Before you eat a piece of this, you need to make*
*sure you've got a designated driver with you.*

6 to 8 large tart apples
1 bottle grain alcohol
Pastry for 2-crust pie
1/2 cup sugar
1/2 cup firmly packed dark brown sugar
2 teaspoons flour
1/2 teaspoon nutmeg
1/4 teaspoon cinnamon
1/4 teaspoon allspice
1 tablespoon grated lemon peel
2 tablespoons margarine

Core and pare apples; cut in quarters, then slice thin. Let 'em soak overnight in the grain alcohol. The next day drain 'em. This will improve the taste of the apples and the alcohol when you drink it while you cook. Line 9-inch pie pan with pastry. Mix sugars, flour, and spices. Rub a little sugar mixture onto the pastry in the pan. Arrange apple slices in pan, heapin' slightly in center. Sprinkle evenly with remainin' sugar mixture. Scatter lemon peel over surface. Dot with margarine. Adjust to crust; trim edges, and flute. Cut slits in center to allow steam to escape. Bake at 425 degrees for 40 to 45 minutes or until apples are tender and pastry golden brown.

—*MOMMA BALLZAK, LOT #16*

## PREMIUM DELUXE HOT FUDGE PIE

*This used to be known as Eula's Hot Fudge Pie. All Mable did was add an additional half-teaspoon of imitation vanilla extract to Eula's recipe, and now it has magically become "Premium Deluxe." Lord, I tell you, sometimes folks think they're all that and a pizza.*

1/2 cup margarine
2 squares semisweet chocolate
1 cup sugar
2 eggs, lightly beaten
1/4 cup all-purpose flour
1 teaspoon imitation vanilla extract
1/2 teaspoon salt

Preheat the oven to 400 degrees. Grease a 9-inch pie pan. Melt the margarine and chocolate in the top of a double boiler over simmerin' water. After it has melted, take it off the heat, and stir in the sugar. Cool slightly. Stir in the eggs, flour, vanilla, and salt. Pour it into the pie pan. Bake for 15 to 20 minutes or until it sets. Cool slightly on a wire rack and serve. It is great with ice cream.

—*MABLE SKAGGS, LOT #17*

## BUTTERMILK PIE

*Momma won a blue ribbon in 1956 and 1972
with this tasty pie.*

2 sticks margarine, melted
1 cup sugar
4 tablespoons flour
6 eggs
1–2 teaspoons imitation vanilla extract
1 cup buttermilk

Mix all together and bake at 300 degrees until done (approximately 45 minutes to an hour).

—*MOMMA BOXCAR, LOT #5*

## BUTTERSCOTCH PIE

*This is another one of Opal's outstandin' food
items. It's just too bad she'll never have a husband
to cook it for.*

6 beaten egg yolks
3/4 cups granulated sugar
3/4 cups brown sugar
1 1/2 cups half & half
1/4 cup melted margarine
1 teaspoon imitation vanilla extract
few drops almond flavorin'

Mix all ingredients together and pour into an unbaked 9-inch pie shell. Bake about 10 to 20 minutes at 450 degrees to set and start browning crust. Open the oven door until it gets down to 200 degrees, and let it cook till the fillin' sets. It can be served with whipped cream.

—*OPAL LAMB, LOT #14*

## CHERRY CHEESE ICE BOX PIE

*This is a big hit at the Taco Tackle Shack!*

8 oz. package cream cheese
7 oz. sweetened condensed milk (recipe is in the COOKIE section)
1/3 cup lemon juice
1 teaspoon imitation vanilla extract
1 can cherry pie fillin'

Blend cheese and milk; add lemon juice and imitation vanilla extract. Pour into 9-inch graham cracker crust and chill 2 or 3 hours. Before servin', pour cherry pie fillin' over top.

—*LOIS BUNCH, LOT #3*

## CHEERY CHERRY COBBLER PIE

*I don't know why Kitty calls this a cobbler and a pie, but I also don't know why she owns Slim Whitman albums either. In any case, here it is.*

*Makes 4 servings*

16 oz. can cherry pie fillin'
1 teaspoon lemon juice
1/3 cup margarine
1/4 cup brown sugar
1 cup flour
3/4 teaspoon cinnamon
1/4 teaspoon allspice
1/2 cup chopped walnuts
1/2 pint vanilla ice cream

Combine cherry pie fillin' and lemon juice; mix well. Turn into an ungreased bakin' dish. Blend margarine, brown sugar, flour, cinnamon, and allspice with fingers until crumbly. Work in walnuts. Sprinkle over cherry fillin'. Heat in microwave oven for 5 to 7 minutes, until cobbler is bubbly. Spoon into individual dishes and top with ice cream.

—*KITTY CHITWOOD, LOT #11*

## MOMMA'S CHESS PIE

*This is the recipe that got me turned into a chess pie junkie.*

3 eggs
1 1/2 cups sugar
1/3 cube margarine
1/4 cup milk
1 teaspoon imitation vanilla extract
2 tablespoons corn meal
A baked pie shell

Beat the eggs, and add the sugar, margarine (melted), milk, vanilla, and corn meal. Continue beatin' until it is well mixed. Pour into pie shell. Bake at 325 degrees for 45 minutes to 1 hour.

—*MOMMA BOXCAR, LOT #5*

## RUBY ANN BOXCAR'S CHESS PIE

*I can eat this stuff till it makes me vomit. God, do I love chess pie!*

3 egg yolks
3/4 cup sugar
1/2 cup of margarine, softened
3 tablespoons heavy cream
Pinch nutmeg
Pinch salt
A baked pie shell

Beat the egg yolks until they get thick and lemon-colored. Beat in the sugar, margarine, cream, nutmeg, and salt. Pour into pie shell, and bake at

350 degrees for 35 minutes. Cool completely before servin'. Before you take a bite of this food of the gods, let me give you a one word warnin', "MILK!"

—*RUBY ANN BOXCAR, LOT #18*

## CHOCOLATE PIE

*As you can tell by the measurements, this is a non-school recipe.*

1/2 cup margarine
3/4 cup sugar
2 squares unsweetened chocolate
2 eggs
2 cups whipped cream
1 cup COCOA PUFFS
A baked pie shell

Cream margarine and sugar. Melt the chocolate and add to creamed mixture. Beat in the eggs one at a time, chill well. Fold in whipped cream. Pour into pie shell. Sprinkle the COCOA PUFFS on top. Keep well chilled.

—*OLLIE WHITE, LOT #10*

## BEST EVER CHOCOLATE PIE

*This is my second favorite pie that my momma makes. It won her a blue ribbon back in 1963 at the Arkansas State Fair.*

11/2 cups sugar
4 heapin' teaspoons flour
1/4 teaspoon salt
3 heapin' tablespoons cocoa
Mix and add:
1 cup cold water

Mix and add:

3 beaten egg yolks

1 cup hot water

Cook until thick. Remove from heat and add:

1 tablespoon margarine

1/2 teaspoon imitation vanilla extract

A baked pie crust

Pour into the crust on page 198 and top with meringue and allow to cool slightly.

—*MOMMA BOXCAR, LOT #5*

## QUICK CHOCOLATE PIE

*Lulu Bell came up with this pie while tryin' to re-create my momma's award-winnin' chocolate pie.*

1 small pkg. chocolate instant puddin'

1 cup cold milk

2/3 cup sweetened condensed milk (recipe is in the COOKIE section)

1 small container whipped cream

Graham cracker crust

1/2 cup chopped nuts (optional)

Pour puddin' mix into mixin' bowl, add milk and beat at lowest speed, until well blended. Add condensed milk and mix well. Fold in whipped cream and pour into a vanilla wafer crust or graham cracker crust and chill. Nuts maybe added for variation.

—*LULU BELL BOXCAR, LOT #8*

## AMAZIN' SECRET COCONUT PIE

*The secret is it makes its own crust.*

2 cups milk

3/4 cup sugar

1/2 cup BISQUICK
4 eggs
1/4 cup margarine
1 1/2 teaspoons imitation vanilla extract
1 cup angel flake coconut

Combine milk, sugar, BISQUICK, eggs, margarine, and imitation vanilla extract in blender or mixer. Mix well. Pour into a well-greased 9-inch pie pan. Let stand 5 minutes, then sprinkle with the coconut. Bake at 350 degrees for 40 minutes. Serve warm or cold. Also makes a good chocolate pie: Mix 3 tablespoons cocoa with the same method and leave off the coconut, if desired.

—*JUANITA HIX, LOT #9*

## MOMMA'S AWARD-WINNIN' COCONUT CREAM PIE

*The 1947 County Fair blue ribbon was given to this pie. I make it every two or three months, but my husband, Dew, doesn't care for coconut. Not bein' one to throw away good food, I usually end up eatin' the whole thing.*

1 cup sugar
3 tablespoons flour
2 large eggs
1/2 cup sweet condensed milk (recipe is in the COOKIE section)
1 cup milk
1 cup coconut
1 teaspoon imitation vanilla extract
9-inch baked pie crust

Mix the sugar and flour together real well. Separate the eggs. Beat the yolks slightly, and mix them with the condensed milk. Add the milk to this mixture, and then add all of this to the sugar/flour mixture. Mix well. Put it in a pot over low heat, and cook until it thickens. Add the coconut and vanilla to the heated mixture. Remove it from the heat, and stir it until it's smooth. Pour it into the pie crust. Beat the egg whites until they're stiff. Add 3 tablespoons of sugar, and spread it on top. Mix together 1/4 cup of coconut and 1 teaspoon of sugar. Spread this mixture on top of the last. Serve warm or cold with a big glass of milk.

*—MOMMA BOXCAR, LOT #5*

# DORA'S OLD-FASHION EGG CUSTARD PIE

*There's been a feud goin' on for many years as to if this an actual old-fashion egg custard pie recipe or not. Everybody in the park has their own feelin's on this topic. Of course, around rent time, everybody but Nellie Tinkle says it is. Did I mention the fact that Nellie and her husband C.M. own their lot outright?*

3 large eggs
1 pie crust
3/4 cup sugar
1/4 teaspoon salt
1 teaspoon imitation vanilla extract
2 cups milk
1/2 teaspoon nutmeg

Preheat the oven at 425 degrees before you do anything else. Beat eggs slightly and brush the bottom of crust with a little bit of the eggs. Let the crust dry in the refrigerator. Add sugar, salt, vanilla, and milk to the remainin' eggs. Mix well. Pour into the refrigerated pie crust, and sprinkle with nutmeg. Place the pie on the lowest rack in the stove, and bake at 325 degrees for 40 minutes.

*—DORA BEAVER, LOT #7*

# NELLIE'S "AUTHENTIC" OLD-FASHION EGG CUSTARD PIE

*Seein' how Nellie's a breath away from the grave,
I tend to believe this is the real old-fashion egg
custard pie recipe.*

*Makes 2 pies*
5 eggs
2 tablespoons flour
1 cup sugar
2 cups sweetened condensed milk (recipe is in the COOKIE section)
2 tablespoons margarine
1 teaspoon imitation vanilla extract
2 pie crusts

Beat the eggs and add the flour and sugar. Mix well. Make sure the sugar and flour are thoroughly mixed before addin' it to the eggs. Add the condensed milk and margarine, and then pour mixture into unbaked, un-egged, unrefrigerated pie crusts. Bake at 450 degrees for 15 minutes. Reduce the heat to 350 degrees and bake for an additional 25 minutes. The center will be soft, but it will set later.

*—NELLIE TINKLE, LOT #4*

# EGG NOG PIE

*I make this around Christmastime, one for each
of the 12 days of Christmas. Did I mention that
my husband, Dew, doesn't like Egg Nog either?*

1 package unflavored gelatin
1/4 cup cold water
1/3 cup sugar
2 tablespoons cornstarch
1/4 teaspoon salt
2 cups egg nog

1 teaspoon imitation vanilla extract
1 tablespoon rum extract
1 cup whippin' cream
Prebaked chocolate pie crust

Sprinkle gelatin over the water to soften. Mix together the sugar, corn-starch, and salt. Gradually stir in the egg nog. Cook in a pot over medium heat, stirrin' constantly, until it's thick (about 2 minutes). Take it off the heat, and stir in the softened gelatin until it dissolves. Add the vanilla and rum extracts. Chill until it slightly thickens. Take the whippin' cream and whip it until it thickens. Fold it into the egg nog mixture, and spread it in the pie crust. Let it chill until it sets.

—*RUBY ANN BOXCAR, LOT #18*

## JEFFERSON DAVIS PIE

*This was Laverne Lamb's momma's recipe. Ac-cordin' to Dottie, when Dixie Snow Lamb was alive she would make this pie every year on Jeffer-son Davis's birthday. It was Laverne's daddy, Robert E. Lamb, that officially changed the name of Razorbacks Road to Jefferson Davis Boulevard when he was the mayor of Pangburn (1941 to 1952). Dottie has added this pie to her large line of dessert items, which she sells by the piece at the Lamb Department Store.*

3 cups white sugar
1 cup margarine
1 tablespoon flour
1/4 cup salt
1 teaspoon imitation vanilla extract
4 eggs, lightly beaten
1 cup milk
1 unbaked pie crust

Cream the sugar and margarine. Blend the flour, salt, and vanilla together in a small bowl, and beat well. Add the eggs and milk, and then stir in the sugar mixture. Pour the mixture into the pie crust, and bake at 450 degrees for 10 minutes. Reduce the heat to 350 degrees and bake for an additional 30 minutes.

*—DOTTIE LAMB, LOT #14*

## LULU BELL'S LEMON CHESS PIE

*Lulu Bell came up with this recipe just for me. Every year, she bakes one of these pies of the gods for my birthday, me and my husband's anniversary, and at Christmas. She and Dottie Lamb have been negotiatin' on sellin' this in the department store.*

1 3/4 cups sugar
1 tablespoon flour
1/4 teaspoon salt
1 tablespoon cornmeal
4 eggs
1/4 cup milk
1/4 cup margarine, melted
1/4 cup lemon juice
1 tablespoon lemon rind, grated
1 teaspoon lemon extract
1 unbaked pie shell

Mix the first 4 ingredients together. Add the rest of the ingredients and beat until they're thoroughly mixed. Pour into the shell and bake at 350 degrees for 40 minutes.

*—LULU BELL BOXCAR, LOT #6*

## OATMEAL PIE

*This is my husband's great aunt Tiffany Addams's recipe. His Aunt Tiffany and her daughter, Lila Bell, operate a wig stylin' and dog groomin' shop in San Antonio. Lila Bell is hopin' to someday be in the Olympics. She's been practicin' in the water sports competitions.*

3 eggs, well beaten
3/4 cup sugar
1 cup brown sugar
2 tablespoons margarine
2/3 cup quick-cookin' oatmeal
1 tablespoon imitation vanilla extract

Mix everything together and pour it into an uncooked pie shell. Bake at 350 degrees for 40 to 45 minutes. Sprinkle some powdered sugar on the top for decoration.

—*RUBY ANN BOXCAR, LOT #18*

## PECAN PIE

*Nellie has always said she'd take this recipe with her to the grave. This is all because of a fight she and Dora had concernin' who made the best pecan pie. Luckily she had a terrible case of stomach flu one day while I was visitin'! Never leave a fat gal alone in your kitchen with all your recipes for any amount of time.*

3 eggs
1 cup white syrup
1/2 cup sugar
3/4 cup sweetened condensed milk (recipe is in the COOKIE section)
1 tablespoon margarine, melted

1 teaspoon imitation vanilla extract

1 cup pecans

1 unbaked pie shell

Beat the eggs, and then add the syrup, sugar, milk, and margarine. Mix well. Add the vanilla. Put the pecans in the bottom of the pie crust. Pour on the mixture, and bake at 350 degrees for 45 minutes. The pecans will rise to the top while cookin'.

—*NELLIE TINKLE, LOT #4*

## DORA'S GOOD AS IT GETS PECAN PIE

*Once again, if you give someone your trailer key so they can feed your cat while you're on vacation, you need to make sure and lock up your recipes.*

8 oz. cream cheese, softened

1/3 cup and 1/4 cup sugar

1/4 teaspoon salt

2 teaspoons imitation vanilla extract

4 eggs

1 unbaked pie shell

1 1/4 cups pecans, chopped

1 cup light corn syrup

In a small bowl combine the cream cheese, 1/3 cup of sugar, salt, 1 teaspoon imitation vanilla extract, and 1 egg. Blend until it's smooth. Spread it in the bottom of the pie crust. Sprinkle on the pecans. Clean the bowl, and combine the remainin' ingredients in it. Mix well. Pour it on top of the pecans, and bake at 375 degrees for 35 to 40 minutes. Let it cool before servin'.

—*DORA BEAVER, LOT #7*

## PUMPKIN PIE

*Lovie cooks like a demon right before Thanks-givin'. She makes 23 of these pies! Every employee at the Pangburn Bugle gets one, and she hands out the other 21 to local Democratic Party officials.*

2 cups cooked pumpkin or pumpkin fillin'
1 cup sweetened condensed milk (recipe is in the COOKIE section)
1/2 teaspoon ginger
1 1/4 cup brown sugar
2 eggs
1 teaspoon cinnamon
1/4 teaspoon nutmeg
1/4 teaspoon imitation vanilla extract
1/2 teaspoon salt
One slightly prebaked pie shell

Combine all the ingredients together and blend thoroughly. Pour into pie shell, and bake for 35 minutes at 350 degrees. Let it cool down and top it with whipped cream.

—*LOVIE BIRCH, LOT #20*

## MOMMA'S RHUBARB CREAM PIE

*I've never cared for the taste of rhubarb. But, everybody always raves about Momma's rhubarb cream pie. I can't tell you it tastes good, but I can tell you it never lasts long at any function that she takes it to.*

1 1/2 cup sugar
3 tablespoons flour
1/2 teaspoon nutmeg
1 tablespoon margarine
2 eggs, well beaten

3 cups rhubarb, cut

1 unbaked pie shell, plus addition pastry for lattice

Blend together all the ingredients except the rhubarb. Put the rhubarb in the bottom of the pie shell, and pour the mixture over the top. Put a lattice of pie pastry on top of this, and bake at 450 degrees for 10 minutes. Reduce the heat to 350 degrees, and bake for an additional 30 minutes.

—*MOMMA BOXCAR, LOT #5*

## STRAWBERRY PIE

*I hear that this will be on the menu at Anita's bar when they start servin' food items.*

1 box strawberry puddin'

1 1/4 cups milk

1/2 cup sweetened strawberries

1/2 cup whipped cream

1 graham cracker crust

Blend the first two ingredients together with an electric mixer (slow speed) until smooth. Add the strawberries, fold in the whipped cream, and spread into the crust.

—*ANITA BIGGON, LOT #2*

## OLLIE'S VIVACIOUS VINEGAR PIE

*This might sound gross, but how can you argue with someone that has several Hairnet Awards on the shelves in her trailer?*

1 cup sugar

2 eggs, beaten

2 tablespoons vinegar

1 cup water

2 tablespoons flour

1/2 teaspoon lemon extract

Small lump of margarine
1 baked pie shell

Cook the sugar, eggs, vinegar, water, and flour in a double boiler until they get thick and smooth. Just before removin' it from the heat, stir in the lemon extract and the lump of margarine. Pour into the pie shell. Cool and top with meringue or whipped cream.

—*OLLIE WHITE, LOT #10*

# Index